Praying
Each Day
of the Year

Nicholas Hutchinson FSC

Matthew James Publishing Ltd

Also available:

 1 898 366 30 6   Praying Each Day of the Year - volume 1: (January - April)
 1 898 366 32 2   Praying Each Day of the Year - volume 3: (September - December)

First published 1998 by:

Matthew James Publishing Ltd,
19 Wellington Close, Chelmsford, Essex CM1 2EE

© 1998 Nicholas Hutchinson FSC

Reprinted 2000

ISBN: 1 898366 31 4

Cover design by Jez Coan
Printed by J W Arrowsmith Ltd, Bristol

*Dedicated
to the memory of
Brother Damian Lundy, FSC
(1944-1996)
who shared the Good News with many
and bore sickness bravely.*

Contents

Foreword

A warm welcome to all who have taken up this book, including many who discovered Volume 1 who are other than teachers - adults using the book for personal prayer; parish leaders accompanying RCIA and other groups; priests and deacons who are keen to incorporate into their homilies an appropriate story; those who are sick or housebound whose prayer for others is much valued.

You are reading the second of three volumes that together offer for every day of the year a reflection and a prayer. The reflection is a "picture-story" - either a story itself or, more often, details of a specific event whose anniversary it is on that day. The accompanying prayer has been written around the theme. The book illustrates very practically how we can reflect on daily life and experiences and, living in God's Presence, can bring everything to him in prayer. It is hoped that the material may be of help in promoting a sense of reflection and prayerfulness that can pervade the day.

In 1997 a draft version of the book was used in different ways across the country in various schools, homes and parishes, but the book is written in the first instance for use by teachers in secondary schools. Teachers have "tried and tested" much of the material, and I have been very grateful for their comments and suggestions, as also those of various individuals who have used the draft version of the book for their personal reflection and prayer each day, especially several people who are seriously ill. Someone has remarked that "the reflective and prayerful approach of the book clearly proclaims that Jesus is the Way, the Truth and the Life".

Produced after much research, the book is offered primarily to busy Form Tutors who don't normally have much time or access to good resources to be producing more than a prayer as the *daily act of collective worship*" for their own class at the start of each day. Teachers have commented already that this book offers ready-to-use quality material that helps to promote a sense of awareness, wonder and appreciation, that can contribute to the personal and spiritual development of individuals.

May all who use this book find help in reflecting and praying and walking in God's presence each day.

Introduction

The value of "picture-stories"

The most famous of all photographs of the Vietnam War was the horrific scene of several children suffering from the effects of napalm, pictured as they were running along a road, towards the camera. It is recognised that the photograph, taken in August 1972 and seen by millions throughout the world, was instrumental in bringing the war to an end. How powerful a picture can be! For hundreds of years, stained-glass windows presented picture-images mainly to those who could not read the Bible. Through her TV programmes and her books, Sister Wendy Becket has helped many people to *"really see"* and understand various meanings in paintings, illustrating the insight of D.H.Lawrence that *"the sense of wonder is the sixth sense, and it is the natural religious sense."* Saint Augustine has said that *"our whole business in this life is to restore to health the eye of the heart by which God may be seen"*, and we acknowledge that Christian education should promote in people *"a way of seeing"* (Evelyn Underhill), developing what William Blake calls *"the inward eye".*

Stories, too, can be "pictures" that convey a profound message, bringing it all alive. Aesop's fables have remained popular for 2,600 years. The Brothers Grimm recorded such stories as 'Little Red Riding Hood', teaching in a subtle way the need for personal safety. "Picture-stories" can also serve as "hooks" on which to "hang" what may be significant to an individual. Jesus told stories as a means of conveying the deep - yet simple - message of the Good News. That great story-writer, Charles Dickens, remarked that *"the Parable of the Prodigal Son is the best short story in the English language"* - not simply because of the poetry of the words, but because it is a timeless story that can reveal more each time it is heard. Some of Dickens' own stories portrayed a "hidden message" of the need for social change.

Some of the best stories are those that leave questions for the individual to ponder, and so can be more powerful in conveying a message than can an 'explanation' that attempts to summarise the message, just as adverts that leave something to the imagination are the most effective. It has been said that *"Jesus told stories and asked questions; we tend to moralise and give answers!"* It is hoped that each day's reflection and prayer will leave people with questions to ask of themselves in looking upon life critically and creatively, as well as leading them in ways of praying. The material in the book focuses on the specific rather than on what is general, and may encourage people to be reflective and prayerful based on the "here and now" of their daily lives. Some have commented that they have gained insights into how items from the news and newspapers can readily be turned to reflection and prayer.

Growing in awareness of the Presence of God

As the mind wanders during the day, it is likely that a recent "picture-story" is thought of again, encouraging the individual to reflect further. This thoughtfulness can, in turn, become part of a growing sense of being in the Presence of God. *"Prayer is about awakening to the Presence of God within us"* (Laurence Freeman), and *"the more we find Christ within, the more we become aware of Christ without"* (Bede Griffiths). As our young people are encouraged to acknowledge and recognise God's presence in themselves and in others, their lives and the lives of those around them will be enriched. It is true to say that the more we place ourselves in God's Presence, the more likely we are to have the same attitude and actions as Jesus: *"In his Presence we are bound to love"* (Evelyn Underhill).

The witness of reflection and prayer

Occasionally we experience or read about how an individual praying in great sincerity has a profound effect on others, and we can recall Pope Paul VI's memorable words:

People *"today listen more willingly to witnesses than to teachers, and if they do listen to teachers, it is because they are witnesses."*

(Evangelii Nuntiandi, 41)

Twice in his weekly articles in 'The Tablet', John Harriot reflected on Brother Alphonsus, a De La Salle Brother who had taught him. Harriot wrote of: *"the effect of seeing him pray and how he seemed to make God visible. Unobtrusively, unselfconsciously, the faith that inspired him was woven in and out of all he did. He was not given to pious exhortations. His pulpit was himself. Above all he was the kindest and gentlest of men."* ('The Tablet': 14/4/90). He went on to write about how Alphonsus was one of many who quietly and perseveringly lived his faith and made it real to all who came under his influence.

The crime-writer, Agatha Christie, wrote in her autobiography:

I can picture one teacher there - I can't recall her name.
She was short and spare, and I remember her eager jutting chin.
Quite unexpectedly one day
(in the middle, I think, of an arithmetic lesson)
she suddenly launched forth on a speech on life and religion.
"All of you," she said,
"every one of you, will pass through a time when you will face despair.

If you never face despair,
you will never have faced, or become, a Christian, or known a Christian life.
To be a Christian
you must face and accept the life that Christ faced and lived:
you must enjoy things as he enjoyed things,
be as happy as he was at the marriage at Cana,
know the peace and happiness that it means
to be in harmony with God and with God's will.
But you must also know, as he did,
what it means to be alone in the Garden of Gethsemane,
to feel that all your friends have forsaken you,
that those you love and trust have turned away from you,
and that God himself has forsaken you.
Hold on then to the belief that that is not the end.
If you love, you will suffer,
and if you do not love, you do not know the meaning of a Christian life."
She then returned to the problems of compound interest
with her usual vigour,
but it is odd that those few words,
more than any sermon I ever heard, remained with me
and, years later, they were to come back to me and give me hope
at a time when despair had me in its grip.
*She was a dynamic figure and also, I think, a **fine** teacher;*
I wish I could have been taught by her longer.

[Agatha Christie: 'An Autobiography'
(William Collins, 1977) page 150]

Both examples are of teachers who reflected on their personal experiences, and shared insights with the young people entrusted to their care - reflections that would bear fruit in years to come.

Good schools promote and cultivate goodness, and we are invited to fill our minds and share with others those things that are *"noble and good, praiseworthy and right, honourable and inspiring"* (Phil 4[4-9]). This book offers in a clear form many insights from our heritage that can be shared and passed on to others - insights that may be of lasting value to our students as they face the challenge to review their priorities. The reflections are presented in ways that attempt to engage interest and imagination during our *"daily act of collective worship"* in school (The Education Reform Act, 1988, s.6).

Some teachers will be of other than the Catholic faith, and some may choose to involve the students fully in the giving of the reflection and prayer. In time to come, the practice of reflecting and praying may develop in such a way that members of the school community from the youngest to the oldest may be able to share with others the fruits and insights of their own reflection and reading and life-experience and, in God's Presence, bring everything together in prayer. The following words of Pope Paul VI refer to people of all ages:

Above all, the Gospel must be proclaimed by witness.
Take a Christian, or a handful of Christians
who, in the midst of their own community,
show their capacity for understanding and acceptance,
their sharing of life and destiny with other people,
their solidarity with the efforts of all
for whatever is noble and good.
Let us suppose that, in addition,
they radiate in an altogether simple and unaffected way
their faith in values that go beyond current values,
and their hope in something that is not seen
and that one would not dare to imagine.
Through this wordless witness,
these Christians stir up irresistible questions
in the hearts of those who see how they live:
Why are they like this?
Why do they live in this way?
What or who is it that inspires them?
Why are they in our midst?
Such a witness is already
a silent proclamation of the Good News,
and a very powerful and effective one.

(Evangelii Nuntiandi, 21)

Young people need an experience of reflection and prayer.

In today's society with vast knowledge at our fingertips, we need to be careful to avoid "information overload". Peter Walker, a former Secretary of State for Wales, remarked that the hour he set aside every morning simply to reflect and "think his thoughts", with no distractions around him, enabled him to keep everything in perspective and be creative. That extraordinary man, Nelson Mandela, said: *"Although it was a tragedy to spend twenty-seven years in prison, one of the advantages was the ability to sit down and think. This is one of the things I miss most."*

The Book of Proverbs tells us that, *"Where there is no vision, the people perish"* (29[18]), reminding us of Plato's words that *"the unreflected life is* not worth living." Jesus *"offered reflections on every aspect of daily life"*, Pope John Paul remarked during his visit to Scotland (1/6/82). The book illustrates how we can reflect on daily life. Reflections can then be brought together in prayer in the same way as the "collecting" of thoughts and intentions in the prayer that was once called the "Collect" in the Eucharist. The material in this book offers the all-important perspective of unity of life and human experience, seeking to integrate daily life rather than fragment and compartmentalise into "sacred" and "secular". Reflecting and praying may help to clarify our vision, review our priorities, and gain insights into how to learn from our experiences, as well as growing in Christ.

'Praying Each Day of the Year' may help in introducing some students to a spiritual life. Respecting the autonomy of each person, use of this book offers an experience of reflection and prayer in which some of the young people will participate fully. Some students may find it interesting or helpful to 'observe' people praying. Others may, in time, *"pray in their inner room"* (Mt 6⁶) and *"seek first the kingdom of God"* (Mt 6³³). Some may take away "seeds" that may come to fruition only in the Lord's good time - not necessarily in ours!

The sharing of a reflection and prayer can be one of the means of Christian formation and a powerful means for people to grow. This particular sharing is an aspect of one of the key elements in pastoral care - wanting to *"be with"* the young people and hoping to *"touch (or win) their hearts"*, offering an opportunity and an invitation to grow. The quality of a teacher's *"being with"* reflects the beliefs that the teacher has for the students, and has an impact on what the young people think of themselves. Indeed, one expression of *"invitational teaching"* is for the teacher to give his or her students *"a vision of their own greatness"* (Pullias).

"You send strange invitations, Sir," says Beauty in 'Beauty and the Beast'. Reflecting and praying with others can be a means of extending "invitations":

- invitations to grow in respect and appreciation of self and others;
- invitations to grow in responsibility, and serve those in need;
- invitations to grow in awareness and wonder, in understanding
  and wisdom (*"Wonder is the seed of knowledge"* remarked Francis Bacon);
- invitations to gain insights into what is of real value, and be life-affirming;
- invitations to discover *"the kingdom within"*, seeking *"life in all its fullness"* as Jesus promised, becoming *"fully alive"* for the glory of God (cf. St Irenaeus).

Indeed, we read in *"The Common Good"* (of the Bishops' Conference of England and Wales, 1996 [37]) that

> *"it is the destiny and duty of each human being*
> *to become more fully human."*

Teaching itself is a way of *"being with"* people, and can include a mutual accompanying on the journey of growing in faith (cf. Emmaus: Lk 24[13-35]). Sometimes we have responded inadequately to young people's thirst for religious experience, yet *"it is necessary that the young know Christ who walks.... alongside each person as a friend"* (Pope John Paul II: 'Crossing the Threshold, p126). Use of this book offers an opportunity for people to walk in God's Presence.

Use in school

Many teachers will attest to the value of praying briefly **for** the students before praying **with** them - whether taking a moment to pray for them on the way to school or whilst walking to class, being conscious that *"if the Lord does not build the house, it is in vain that the builders labour."* (Ps 127[1]). We place our trust in the Lord to whom one of his friends said: *"Lord, teach us to pray"* (Lk 11[1]).

"The daily acts of collective worship" are part of the shared mission of the whole school community, whether they take place as class assemblies or larger group assemblies. As with various pastoral initiatives in secondary schools, if the sharing of a reflection and prayer is started as Year 7 arrive, they will assume it is the usual practice, and so will accept it as the norm for future years.

It is necessary to read through the material at least a day in advance. You may reflect on it personally yourself, and then have other ideas to contribute, so that it will become a personal reflection on your part. On days when it is decided to use the material in the format given, the numbering of each paragraph lends itself to the active participation of several people. If others are to be involved in the sharing of the reflection and prayer, you will want to encourage their preparation of the material in advance. Sometimes teachers take it for granted that readings will be presented clearly, with sufficient volume, and slowly enough! Do alert readers to any unusual words. The fact that students lead or present part of the reflection and prayer may also become one of the means for their growth in self-confidence and self-esteem.

If the prayer to be used is short, it is advisable for it to be written in advance on the board or for use with the overhead projector (prepared in either case before the students are in the room). A sense of involvement and participation and "ownership" is increased if everyone is invited to make such vocal prayer together, and we know that what is visual (in this case, the written word) is understood and retained much longer than what is simply heard. Such a visual stimulus encourages recall and further reflection later in the day.

Many of us have tended to limit ourselves to use only two or three 'formal' prayers as public prayer. Profound as those prayers are, the young people will not necessarily experience that prayer can be 'worded' in a way that is specific to situations in their daily lives. Prayer can be informal and familiar, and Carlo Carretto reminds us that *"prayer takes place in the heart, rather than in the head."* Deliberately the prayers here have not been written in formal or polished English, but generally in the style of spoken English. It is hoped that the style of the prayers will help promote the "speaking from the heart" that prayer is. Having read and used some of the prayers in this book, prayer-leaders may well feel encouraged to extemporise prayer in public, or write down words in advance that will be used as prayer.

On some days a quote or "punchline" may be repeated after the prayer - all the more effective if the prayer-leader avoids making an additional comment, thereby tending to elicit a personal response from some when recalled later in the day. To attempt to "preach" what kind of response there "should" be is likely to put people off and limit the action of the Holy Spirit!

Not all teachers fully appreciate that all the positive elements of a reflection and prayer can be negated by the attitude of one of the prayer-leaders or by the delivery or manner of delivery of comments or notices that might follow.

For those who wish (and have the time) to use the material more extensively (whether for a longer time in class, or for a year or school assembly), additional background information and some biblical references are included at the end of most days (📖). These details may help both teachers and students to introduce further ideas, and the cross-referring between some days may be of help. The additional background information is also there to help promote the thirst for knowledge, wisdom and understanding in the young people who themselves read the material, possibly following up by using CD-ROM encyclopedias, etc.

Teachers will find that materials set out for weekends and for holiday times - particularly the month of August - will provide further resource material for use on school days!

For year or school assemblies, some hymns are listed to offer a ready choice, suitable to the theme of the day (🎼). Occasionally reference is made to a poem. Such poems are the more commonly known and, for convenience, all are to be found in *"The Nation's Favourite Poems"* (BBC Books 0-563-38782-3), being a compilation of the nation's top 100 favourite poems, according to a Radio 4 nationwide poll in 1995.

'Praying Each Day of the Year' is printed in three conveniently-sized volumes. At the back of the appropriate volume appear materials for such "movable feasts" as Ash Wednesday, the days of Holy Week, Pentecost, and Family Fast Days. The book's comprehensive index should help to locate themes, people, and particular passages, especially if you recall only a few key words of a familiar passage.

Many will find very useful a resource that is printed at the back of Volume 1 -*"Locating passages in the Bible"*, with references to some 600 key events and writings from both the Old and the New Testaments, listed in a very clear and user-friendly way. Too often we have thought of a passage but have been unable to locate it! Many of the prayers in the book have drawn their inspiration from scripture.

At the back of this volume is a collection of prayers for use by teachers for colleagues and students. These have been "tried and tested" by several schools which now choose one of these (or other) prayers for staff briefings and meetings, for the daily or weekly staff briefing sheet, for the monthly newsletter to parents, or for such occasions as the annual parent-governor meeting. Individual teachers have used the collection as a means of praying for colleagues and for particular students.

Volume 3 concludes with various means for helping people to recall that we are in the Presence of God.

As you take up this book each day, it will be in the spirit of all that is presented here if, briefly, you think and pray for all others in different schools and situations who will be using the same material as you. Do pray that we may all become more reflective and prayerful and *"fully alive"* because we have shared an experience of something of God's love. And so may all of us who use this book - fellow pilgrims on the road to Emmaus - each be able to share our own story of what happens to us on our journey through life, and how we recognise Jesus in our midst.

Brother Nicholas Hutchinson, FSC
De La Salle House,
83 Carr Lane East,
Liverpool L11 4SF

Praying
Each Day
of the Year

1   In 1889, the date of 1st May was settled upon as the day to celebrate across the world the achievements and hopes of workers. May Day became particularly significant in Communist countries, and a Parade was held to praise political leaders and display military tanks, missiles and planes.

2   Before the collapse of Communism in the late 1980s and early 1990s, Moscow - the capital of the then Soviet Union - held the greatest of all military parades. At the 1954 May Day Parade in Red Square in Moscow, American observers saw what they thought was a huge fleet of long-range nuclear bombers flying overhead, one by one.

3   In fact there were only 4 such bombers. Again and again each plane roared over Red Square and then flew over the horizon before travelling back round again, out of sight. Because the 4 planes were equally spaced, they gave the impression of a huge fleet of these nuclear bombers, flying over one by one. During the following 3 years, America spent millions of dollars building fighter planes that could intercept what they thought were many nuclear bombers. Then it was discovered that the Soviet nuclear threat actually lay in missiles, and so Western countries began to spend more and more, producing their own missiles. This was part of *"the Arms Race"*, wasting more and more money and resources.

4   As it was Communism that focussed particularly on 1st May as the Workers' Day, Pope Pius XII *(the twelfth)* in 1955 declared the same day to be the feast of Saint Joseph the Worker. Joseph (a carpenter) is the patron saint of all working people.

5   *Let us pray:*

> **On this day, Lord,**
>   **we can celebrate**
>   **many achievements of humanity**
> **as a whole,**
> **but never let us forget**
> **that each and every individual**
> **needs to be held in respect.**
> **We pray today for the unemployed**
> **and for those unable to work,**
> **and we ask you to give success**
> **to the work of our hands. Amen.**

📖 *It was the 1889 International Socialist Congress in Paris that decided upon the date of 1st May.*

📖 *Pope John Paul II, on his Visit to Britain, spoke in Coventry [30/5/82], a city that had been very heavily bombed during the Second World War:* "The voices of Christians join with others in urging the leaders of the world to abandon confrontation and to turn their backs on policies which require the nations to spend vast sums of money for weapons of mass destruction... Mistrust and division between nations begin in the hearts of individuals. Work for peace starts when we listen to the urgent call of Christ: 'Repent and believe in the Gospel'."

📖 *Psalm 89^{17}: Give success to the work of our hands, Lord.*
Mt 25$^{14-30}$: Good or poor use of people's talents.
2 Thess 3$^{6-12,16}$: Some of you are living in idleness; anyone who refuses to work should not be given any food.

🎵   All that I am; Come let us go up to the Lord; I am with you for ever *(all who labour)*; I give my hands; Lord, make me a means; Lord of all hopefulness *(verse 2 refers to labouring)*; Make me a channel; Peace, perfect peace; Take my hands; Thank you for fathers

2 MAY

1 In 1972, George Lucas, a young film director, planned a film that would be called 'American Graffiti'. Two film companies rejected it. A third turned it down but then had a change of mind. 'American Graffiti' became one of the films that has brought in the most money at "the box office", as people bought their tickets.

2 Despite the great success of his first film, George Lucas had great difficulty getting financial backing from film companies for his second picture - a science-fiction film, to be called 'Star Wars'. Half-heartedly, 'Twentieth Century Fox' risked some money in backing 'Star Wars', but George Lucas had to raise most of the money himself. He became almost bankrupt, but it meant that he owned the rights to the film and any sequels that might be produced.

3 'Star Wars' opened in the cinemas in this month in 1977 and, in its first year, the film brought in 300 million dollars in the United States alone. Its sequel -'The Empire Strikes Back' - earned 200 million dollars in its first year.

4 Film and computer technology has improved greatly since 'Star Wars' was first produced in 1977. The re-release of the newly-edited film twenty years later in 1997 with new computer-generated images, began to bring in even more money. Many viewers went to see 'Star Wars' at the cinema for the first time.

5 The great success of 'Star Wars' is a reminder of the ideals and vision of individuals, and a reminder that our judgements are not always correct. We are also reminded of the need for us all to have faith in ourselves.

6 *Let us pray:*

God our Father, open our eyes
  to see the vision
  that you have for each of us,
  and lead us to grow in confidence
  in who we are,
  and in the faith
  that you call each of us by name.
Show us how to live in such a way
  that we respect and accept others
  for who they are,
  and do not judge them
  as we ourselves
  do not want to be judged.
Inspire us to be generous
  in praising others
  and in showing appreciation
  for their achievements.
Amen.

❖❖❖❖❖❖❖❖❖❖❖❖❖❖❖❖

 In you, my God; The love/dream I have for you; Yahweh, I know you are near

1 Jack Traynor from Liverpool was called up to be a soldier during the First World War. He was hit in the head by a piece of shrapnel which damaged part of his brain, causing him to start to have epileptic fits.

2 He was posted to the battle-area of Gallipoli in the Middle East where, in May 1915, he was seriously wounded by three bullets from a Turkish machine-gun. Because of his injuries he was given a full pension and was discharged from the army in 1917, a year before the end of the First World War.

3 Six years later Jack travelled to Lourdes, to the Shrine of Our Lady in southern France. Three doctors who accompanied the pilgrims signed a statement that he was epileptic and had lost the use of his legs, and was paralysed in one arm.

4 As is the custom in Lourdes, Jack bathed in the waters that flowed from the spring. Shortly afterwards he felt that he could walk, and he began to experience feelings in the arm that had been paralysed. The same three doctors examined him and confirmed that he could now walk and that he had regained the use of his arm. The doctors also acknowledged that the shrapnel wound in his head, through which his brain could be seen, had completely closed.

5 Jack Traynor returned to Liverpool. Because he was now fit and able, he rejoined the family's coal business. The next time his invalidity war pension arrived, he wrote to let them know that he would no longer need the pension because he was now cured of the serious disabilities. The government department wasn't able to acknowledge miracles, and continued to send the disability pension until he died, aged 64.

6 *Let us pray:*

Lord Jesus,
we read in the Gospels
that you brought healing
and acceptance
to many people,
In your love
stretch out your hands
and touch me
and bring healing and wholeness
in my life. Amen.

✍ *Or use the prayer from 11 February or 28 May.*

✍ *Gallipoli - modern-day 'Gelibolu' - is a town of the Dardanelles, along the waterway connecting the Mediterranean and the Black Sea, and is near the border between European Turkey and Asian Turkey.*

✍ *See also 11 February for some details on Lourdes. The film "The Song of Bernadette", tells of Mary's appearance to Bernadette at Lourdes and the cures that began to take place there. At the end of the film the following words appear on screen:*
"For those who believe in God,
no explanation is necessary.
For those who do not believe in God,
no explanation is possible."

✍ *The Guinness Book of Records mentions that the world's largest ambulances are 18m (59 feet) in length, and are often called "Jumbulances". They transport the sick and handicapped on pilgrimages and holidays throughout Europe, including to Lourdes. The Jumbulances carry 44 patients and staff, and are operated by the ACROSS Trust.*

♪ Christ be beside me; For to those who love God; Holy Virgin by God's decree; If God is for us; Lay your hands

4 MAY

1 In 1933, 4 months after Adolf Hitler became Chancellor of Germany, bonfires were lit in many cities. The bonfires were not made of wood - but of books. Public libraries were looted of any books that some considered "non-German". About a million books were destroyed throughout the country.

2 10 months later, in February 1934, a new version of the Psalms was produced by the Nazis. The Book of Psalms from the Old Testament of the Bible was re-written, removing all references to the Jews. Yet the psalms were the prayers of the Jewish people in particular, and the Bible, of course, is written by people who were Jewish. This is the shortest psalm of the Bible:

3 *Praise the Lord, all you nations.*
Speak to him, all people of the earth,
because his love is great
and he is always faithful.

(Psalm 117)

4 Unlike the attitude of the Nazis, that psalm referred not to one nation only, but to all people.

5 Since the time of Jesus, "anti-Semitism" - hatred for Jews - had become an ingrained attitude in many countries of Christian Europe. Hitler knew there was prejudice already there in Christian society, and so faced little opposition to his policies which eventually led to the murder of 6 million Jews.

6 We'll finish with a prayer written about 1960 by Pope John XXIII *(the twenty-third)* who asks for forgiveness for the prejudice of Christians that gave rise to the murder of Jewish people down the ages:

7 *Let us pray:*

O God, we are conscious
that many centuries of blindness
have blinded our eyes
so that we no longer see the beauty
of your Chosen People.
Across the centuries
our Jewish brothers and sisters
have lain in the blood which we drew
or caused to be shed
by forgetting your love.
Forgive us for the curse
we falsely attached
to their name as Jews.
Forgive us
for crucifying you a second time
in their flesh.
For we knew not what we did. Amen.

1 Britain's history would have been very different if the country had remained linked by land to the rest of Europe, instead of there being that wide strip of water we call the English Channel. In time of war the Channel has protected us from invasion and occupation.

2 The English Channel is 34km (21 miles) wide at its narrowest part across the Strait of Dover. Several attempts have been made to create a tunnel that would link Britain with mainland Europe. Tomorrow, 6th May, is the anniversary of the formal Opening of the Channel Tunnel in 1994. The Queen addressed the French President, Monsieur Mitterand, saying that the two nations complemented each other well, despite individual diversity and age-long rivalry. When uniting in a common cause (such as in the Second World War) unity between the two countries was very successful, she said.

3 The building of the Channel Tunnel reminds us to focus on what unites people rather than on what separates and divides.

4 *Let us pray:*

Lord,
> **lead us to be peace-makers,**
> **building connections**
> **between individuals,**
> **focusing on what unites people**
> **rather than on what separates us**
> **and highlights our differences.**

Lord, it's easy to harm relationships;
instead,
> **give us the power of your Spirit**
> **that we may build up and make new**
> **the bonds between people.**

Amen.

✍ *The Channel Tunnel was opened by Queen Elizabeth II and President Mitterand of France on 6/5/97. In French "the English Channel" is called "La Manche" which means "the sleeve", being an "arm" of the Atlantic Ocean.*

✍ *In Shakespeare's 'Richard II', Richard talks of England, valuing the existence of the English Channel:*
> "This fortress built by Nature for herself
> Against infection and the hand of war...
> Or as a moat defensive to a house
> Against the envy of less happier lands."

- Act 2, Scene 1, Line 40.

♪ Christ is our king; Do not be afraid; I will be with you; O Lord all the world belongs to you; Oh the love of my Lord (*"at the turn of each tide"*); You shall cross the barren desert (*"raging waters in the sea"*)

6 MAY

1 No-one could run a mile in under 4 minutes until this day in 1954, when 25-year old Roger Bannister ran a mile in 3 minutes 59.4 seconds in Oxford. It was a very significant achievement. Since then a few people have beaten his record. In 1985 another British athlete, Steve Cram, took the world-record for the mile in 3 minutes 46.32 seconds in Oslo, Norway.

2 The record-breaking Roger Bannister, who later became a medical doctor, wrote a book called *"First Four Minutes"*. We'll listen to some of his words:

3 *"Sooner or later in sport we run into situations that are too big for us to master. In real life we can dodge them. We can play hide and seek with reality, never facing the truth about ourselves. In sport we cannot. It shakes our roots with its confusing pattern of success and failure. As a result, sport leads to the most remarkable self-discovery of our limitations as well as of our abilities.*

4 *"We all have ideals, and as we have grown up we have the choice whether to pursue them or to give them up. If we pursue them we may not attain them. At times we may wonder whether there is any point in the pursuit, because of the sacrifices involved.*

5 *"We need to strive to achieve more and more, not for purely selfish motives, but because of the recognition of some higher purpose. The aim is to move with the greatest possible freedom towards the realisation of the best within us. This is the quest of a lifetime, and sport plays only a small part in it."*

6 *Let us pray:*

Lord, each of us
has different talents and abilities.
We ask you to inspire us
to discover and develop

the best within us.
Lead us to be
both humble and generous
in praising others
for the good use of their talents.
Amen.

✍ *Or could use the prayer from 13 January or 12 June. See also the ideas about "the best" in 29 May.*

✍ *Now **Sir** Roger Bannister, he was a medical student at the time, and achieved this record at the Iffley Road track in Oxford, as he ran for the University of Oxford. Two friends were his pace-setters: Chris Bracher and Chris Chattaway. The theme of the "pacesetter" is expressed in "The Lord is my pace-setter" - a setting of Psalm 22/23 ["The Lord is my shepherd"] by Toki Miyashima. That prayer can be found in "Words of Comfort" by Daniel Cronin [St Paul Publications], 0-85439-344-7, and also in "Short Prayers for the Long Day" by G & M Harcourt [Fount], 0-00-627865-5.*

✍ *On 26/10/97 the world's first "half-marathon robot" took part in a half-marathon run in Bracknell, Berkshire. The 3-wheeled robot was called "Roger" after Sir Roger Bannister.*

✍ *1 Cor 9^{24-27} - all the runners at a race are trying to win; I train hard.*

✍ *Tennyson's poem 'Ulysses' ends with the words, "to strive, to seek, to find, and not to yield."*

♪ Christ be beside me *(pacesetter)*; O Lord all the world belongs to you; Though the mountains may fall *("you will run, never tire")*; Walk with me, O my Lord; Yahweh I know you are near *("where can I run from your love?")*

1 One of the world's greatest musicians, Ludwig van Beethoven, began to lose his hearing when he was only 26. This was particularly tragic for someone so gifted in using sound as music. When he realised he could not be cured of his deafness, he wrote the following prayer. As we hear his words, we can pray for those who are going through difficulties at this time:

2 **O God, give me strength**
   to be victorious over myself.
   O guide my spirit
   and raise me up
   from these dark depths,
   so that
   I may fearlessly struggle upward
   in fiery flight.
   For it is you alone, Lord,
   who understand me
   and can inspire me. Amen.

3 Part of Beethoven's 9th Symphony (which is called "The Choral") has become the Anthem of today's E.U. - the European Union. When this symphony was first performed in Vienna on this day in 1824, Beethoven was completely deaf. During the performance he faced the orchestra and, before each of the four parts (or "movements") of the music, he beat the speed (or "tempo") to let the conductor know how fast the music should be played. In his last years, his only experience of his own music was not through hearing, but through watching the musicians, imagining what they were playing.

4 At the end of this symphony, the audience stood and applauded enthusiastically, but Beethoven could not hear them; someone turned him round to face the audience so that he could see their appreciation of his music.

5 Beethoven's last words before dying are said to have been: *"I will hear in heaven. '*

📖 *In his last years, being totally deaf, Beethoven would depend on what he called his "conversation books" - visitors would write down in these books what they wanted to say in conversation, and then Beethoven would speak a response.*

📖 *For Beethoven, see also 3 March and 28 April.*

📖 *Ludwig van Beethoven: 16/12/1770-26/3/1827.*

🎵 Abide with me; In you my God; I will sing a song; O let all who thirst; Sing a simple song unto the Lord

8 MAY

1 Yesterday, the 7th of May, in 1945, saw the end of the Second World War in Europe. Victory in Europe - or "V.E. Day" was celebrated on this day, the 8th of May.

2 The Second World War continued for another 3 months until Japan surrendered in August 1945.

3 We'll use as our prayer today some words written by Pope Paul VI *(the sixth)* about 25 years later:

4 **Lord, God of peace,**
we thank you for the hopes,
the efforts and the achievements
which your Spirit of peace
has inspired in our days
- stirring up love where there was hate,
sympathy where there was suspicion,
care where there was indifference.

5 **Open our minds and our hearts**
even more
to the specific demands
which love for others makes upon us,
so that we may be more truly
makers of peace.

6 **Remember, God of mercies,**
those who are oppressed,
those who are suffering and dying
for the birth of a world
in which all people
will be more truly
a single human family.

7 **May your kingdom come**
for all people of every race and language
- your kingdom of justice,
of peace, of love,
and may all the earth
be filled with your glory.
We make our prayer
through Jesus Christ,
the Prince of Peace. Amen.

✍ *Could name various parts of the world where there is war, violence, and unrest.*

✍ *Micah 4^{1-4} = Isaiah 2^{1-5} - swords into plough-shares; peace.*

✍ *"V.E Day" - 8th May - marked Victory in Europe. "V.J Day" - 14th August - marked Victory over Japan, bringing the Second World War to an end.*

✍ *Paul VI was Pope from 1963-1978.*

♪ Come let us go up to the Lord; Lord, make me a means of your peace; Make me a channel; Peace, perfect peace

1 "The Red Cross" is known as one of the main international aid agencies. Nowadays The Red Cross is involved in helping when there are disasters such as earthquakes, floods, plane crashes.

2 In time of war, the Red Cross is neutral, providing help to all who need it - for example in Bosnia during and after the civil war there in the 1990s. Missing people can sometimes be traced through the Red Cross. In a war zone, hospital ships and vehicles carrying wounded people often bear a red cross, informing soldiers that they should not fire.

3 How did the Red Cross start? Yesterday, 8th May, is the anniversary in 1828 of the birth of Jean Henri Dunant in Switzerland. Aged 31, in the Franco-Prussian War, he became extremely concerned about the condition of the wounded soldiers he saw. He proposed that there be an international aid agency to help injured soldiers during a time of war.

4 He wanted to choose a flag to represent the organisation, and so he simply reversed the colours of his national flag of Switzerland - the white cross becoming red, and the red background of the Swiss flag becoming white. The 'International Red Cross', as it was called, started in 1864.

5 In countries where the religion is Islam, the same aid agency is called 'The Red Crescent', with its flag of a red crescent-shaped moon on a white background. Whilst the cross is a symbol for Christians, the moon is sometimes a symbol for Muslims (the followers of Islam), and some Islamic countries have a crescent-shaped moon as part of their national flag e.g. Algeria, Pakistan, Singapore, and Turkey.

6 The places where Islam started were desert countries. At night time people would be able to find directions by looking at the position of the moon and the stars. The moon and the stars reminded Muslims that God (Allah) would direct and lead his people.

7 A Muslim once said: *"At night you Westerners see thousands of stars in the sky. We Muslims see only a few stars - and God."*

8 *Let us pray:*

God of all nations and all people,
  inspire us
   to live in your presence each day.
On our journey through life
  lead us to choose
   the right direction,
  and show us
   how to respect and value others,
   even if we do not agree with them.
May we find other people
  as willing to help us
  as we are willing to help them.
Amen.

🖎 *Most of what was Prussia is part of what is now Germany.*

🖎 *In its own words, The Red Cross Society is* "to inspire, encourage and promote at all times, all forms of humanitarian activities... and contribute to the maintenance and promotion of peace." *The British Red Cross, 9 Grosvenor Crescent, London, SW1X 7EJ*

🎵 Christ is our king; Come let us go up to the Lord; Lord, make me a means; Make me a channel; O Lord all the world; Take my hands

1 On this day in 1994 Nelson Mandela was sworn in as the first black President of South Africa. The year before, he and the then President (F.W. de Clerk) jointly received the Nobel Peace Prize for their efforts to establish democracy and racial harmony in their country.

2 Nelson Mandela was elected President 4 years after being released from 27 years' captivity in prison. Two years after his election, Nelson Mandela made a State Visit to Britain. In her Christmas broadcast that year, Queen Elizabeth commented that President Mandela was an inspiration to many people, showing how we can all accept the facts of the past without bitterness, and learn to see new opportunities as more important than differences and disputes of the past.

3 *Let us pray:*

We know, Lord,
   that throughout our lives
   each of us will experience
   problems and difficulties.
Give us courage and strength
   at those times
   and prevent us then
   from looking only at ourselves.
Keep our vision wide
   so that, even in times of difficulty,
   we may still be of help to others.
Help us not to be bitter
   towards people or situations,
   but empower us
   to take the initiative
   and break the cycle
   of hatred, bitterness,
   and evil actions.
Help us to transform
   the difficulties that come our way
   into opportunities for
   personal growth
   and service of others. Amen.

✎ *The word "apartheid" means "separateness" In South Africa other races were kept apar. from the minority white population that gov erned the country.*

✎ *See also 27 April, and 12,18 July.*

🎜 Christ is our king, let the whole world rejoice; God forgave my sin; In you, my God; Lord, make me a means; Make me a channel; My Lord, my Master; O Lord all the world belongs to you

MAY 11

1 Tomorrow, 12th May, is the anniversary in 1935 of the start of "Alcoholics Anonymous". Two men in New York began to support each other to stay sober. "Alcoholics Anonymous" - or "A.A.", as it is often known - has small group meetings in many towns each week. Those who feel they have a drink problem are welcome to attend group meetings, where everyone is anonymous. No one is ever charged money to attend. Members encourage and support one another to live a day at a time.

2 A.A. has *"12 Steps for Recovery"* from alcoholism. Some people who don't have alcohol problems still find A.A.'s 12 *"Steps for Recovery"* to be a good guide when times are difficult. The '12 Steps' include the following:

3 - Realising and admitting that I am powerless over my problem, and have made a mess of my life;

4 - believing that only a Power greater than myself can make me better, so handing my life over to God's care;

5 - taking responsibility for what has gone wrong in the past, and admitting my mistakes to God and to one other person;

6 - asking God to remove my inner problems of character, and bring me healing.

7 *We'll use as our prayer today some words used every day by A.A. members. This prayer is often said together at their group meetings. Let us pray:*

8 **God, grant me the serenity
to accept the things I cannot change,
courage to change the things I can,
and wisdom to know the difference.
Amen.**

✍ *Alcoholics Anonymous adopted this prayer which was written by Reinhold Niebuhr, 1892-1971. "Serenity" is the sense of being at peace.*

✍ *The telephone number of local A.A. groups can be found in the telephone directory under "Alcoholics Anonymous". There are also groups called "Al-Anon for Relatives" for those with a family member with alcohol problems.*

Alcoholics Anonymous,
11 Redcliffe Gardens,
London SW10 9BG.

♪ Amazing grace; Be still and know I am with you; I will never forget you; Lord Jesus Christ, you have come to us *(vv.1,3,4)*; Oh the love of my Lord; O Lord all the world belongs to you

12 MAY

1 In Britain on this day in 1969, the voting age was lowered from 21 to 18.

2 It is a good thing that we should be aware of our rights, but we mustn't lose sight of the fact that, as well as rights, we also have responsibilities and duties towards others.

3 Gandhi, one of India's great leaders, was once presented with a draft Bill of Rights for the people of India. He refused to sign it, saying: *"Show me a bill of **duties** and I will be the first to sign it."*

4 *Let us pray:*

**Lord, remind us
that, along with our rights,
each of us
has duties and responsibilities
towards others. Amen.**

📖 *For 'voting' see 20 January, 14 June, and praye 69 from the Appendix to this volume.*

📖 'Not everything said to be a 'right' really i one. There is no 'right to choose' to harn another, for instance. The proliferation of al leged 'rights' can devalue the very concept So can the amplification of rights withou equivalent stress on duties, and without som concept of the common good to which al have an obligation to contribute."
('The Common Good',36, produced by th Bishops of England & Wales in 1996

📖 *See also 29,30 January and 17 February fo Gandhi.*

📖 *Could adapt and make into a verbal prayer th words of the hymn "Whatsoever you do". A alternative prayer would be that of 26 April.*

🎵 If I am lacking love; I give my hands Make me a channel; O Lord all the world; This is what Yahweh asks of you

1 On this day in 1981 Pope John Paul II was being driven round in his open-topped 'Popemobile', in St Peter's Square in Rome, where about 10,000 people were gathered to see him. He was blessing the crowd when a gunman opened fire and hit the Pope with four bullets, also wounding two other people.

2 Cardinal Hume spoke in London: *"He is now at one with the countless victims of violence of our day. He, like them, has now followed in the footsteps of a Master who was himself so cruelly and callously tortured and killed. He, like his Master, refuses to condemn, and is ready to forgive."*

3 Two years later the Pope had a private meeting in prison with his would-be murderer, Mehmet Ali Agca. Pope John Paul later said: *"I spoke to him as a brother whom I have pardoned."*

4 *Let us pray:*

**Lord, we pray
 for justice and peace in our world.
We pray, too, that those
 who use violence as a weapon
 may be touched
 by the reaction of people
 who have been hurt by violence.
Influence each of us, Lord,
 to bring justice and peace
 to our own part of the world this day.
Amen.**

📁 *After the sudden death of John Paul I, who was Pope for only 33 days, Polish-born Karol Wojtyla was elected Pope on 16/10/1978. During the Second World War, whilst his country was occupied by the Nazis, he trained secretly to become a priest.*

📁 *It was on 27th December 1983 that Mehmet Ali Agca, a Turk, was visited in prison by the Pope. They spoke together for 20 minutes, and the Pope was quizzed by reporters outside, but he said: "What we talked about will have to remain a secret. I spoke to him as a brother whom I have forgiven, and he has my complete trust."*

📁 *Italian Police investigations after the assassination attempt concluded that this was a Communist plot to kill the Polish Pope who, at that time, was of help and inspiration to the people of Poland who would shortly become the first of the Communist-bloc countries to become free. Once Communism fell in Poland, other countries of Eastern Europe and then the Soviet Union itself rapidly gained their freedom in the late 1980s and early 1990s.*

🎵 He said, freely, freely; Lord make me a means; Make me a channel; O Lord all the world; The Lord's my shepherd

14 MAY

1 200 years ago smallpox killed many people. It was a terrible disease and highly contagious, killing 2,000 people every year in London alone.

2 Edward Jenner was aware that people who milked cows caught cowpox, a mild disease. He discovered that no-one who caught cowpox ever caught the deadly smallpox.

3 On this day in 1796 Jenner inoculated an 8-year old boy with cowpox, which is not a serious disease. 6 weeks later he injected the boy with smallpox, but the boy did not become ill. The much milder cowpox had made him immune - he couldn't be hurt by the deadly smallpox.

4 Eventually Jenner's work was appreciated. Giving a mild form of a virus in order to prevent a much worse illness, became known as "vaccination", after the Latin word for "cowpox", recognising that that disease provided the clue to making people immune - resistant - to some serious viral infections.

5 Edward Jenner's work helped save many lives. 100 years later, Louis Pasteur did a lot of work on producing vaccines to prevent other serious illnesses. We now know that an inoculation of a harmless form of a virus causes the human body to produce "antibodies" which stay in the bloodstream, ready to fight against the worst form of the virus if the person becomes infected.

6 Viruses are so tiny that about 40,000 of them, laid end-to-end, would measure a millimetre. Such tiny things can destroy life, just as small things each day - our actions, our attitude - can take life away from other people.

7 *Let us pray:*

Loving Lord,
   I often see on the TV news
   examples of inhumanity to others
   - people being tortured, abused,
   injured or killed.
I need to remind myself
   that the commandment "do not kill"
   also refers to my attitude
   and what I do each day,
   because it is in smaller ways
   that I can destroy people
   if I ignore them
   or cut them off
   or do them down.
Loving Lord, inspire me
   to take care
   of the smaller things of life
   as well as the bigger issues. Amen.

✍ "Contagious" = the spread of disease by direct contact; "infectious" = the spread of disease by air and water.

✍ We may well question Jenner's involvement of another person in his experimental techniques! The 8-year old boy was called James Phipps. Inoculations with smallpox itself had actually been carried out for about 100 years, sometimes curing but often killing patients and starting an epidemic. In 1840 inoculations with smallpox were banned by Parliament, but by then Dr Jenner had discovered that the mild disease of cowpox was a very effective vaccine.

✍ Jenner was the first to make use of the term "**virus**", coming from a Latin word for "poison". Viruses are so small that they can only be seen with a powerful electron microscope. Viruses are the smallest, simplest living things, yet are the cause of some of our deadliest diseases because they replicate by invading host cells and taking over the cell's "machinery" for DNA replication.

✍ **Bacteria** are unicellular micro-organisms and, end-to-end, about 250 bacteria would measure 1 millimetre, and so can be seen with an optical microscope. **Antibiotics** kill bacteria or stop them reproducing; they can't kill viruses which are much smaller, and so antibiotics are useless against colds and flu because they are caused by viruses.

✍ In 1979 the World Health Organisation [W.H.O.] declared that smallpox had been eradicated across the world, and recommended that vaccinations against smallpox no longer be given. They also urged that all laboratory samples of smallpox be destroyed, knowing that there was always a possibility of smallpox escaping from a lab. In the same year, 1979, an Englishwoman had died from smallpox that she contracted whilst working on a sample of the virus in a laboratory.

✍ Edward Jenner: 17/5/1749 - 26/1/1823. For Louis Pasteur see 15,16 July.

✍ Rom 12²¹: Resist evil and conquer it with good.

♪ Abide with me; Father, I place into your hands; If I am lacking love; Lay your hands

15 MAY

1 John Baptist De La Salle was declared the Patron Saint of teachers on this day in 1950.

2 300 years ago, John Baptist De La Salle encouraged teachers to look upon their students as individuals, rather than as a group. He talked of people needing to *"touch hearts"*.

3 *"Touching hearts"* is about acknowledging and relating with people as individuals - helping each person feel that they are noticed and matter, and are significant and special. A personal approach or reaction can make all the difference to an individual, showing that someone is "bothered enough" to care.

4 Someone today can be made to feel "worthwhile" if I call them by their name.

5 I can show human warmth and concern today if I acknowledge individuals with eye-contact, a nod, a smile, or a word.

6 I can *"touch someone's heart"* if I set out to remember what the person says or does. At another time I can repeat those personal details, showing that someone cares enough about them to remember.

7 I can build up people today if I help them to experience success or meaning in their lives, and feel good about themselves.

8 I can help raise someone's self-esteem today if I show that I respect and appreciate that individual and bear in mind their own special circumstances.

9 Someone today can feel valued if I invite them to become part of conversation, to become part of what is going on; setting out to make sure people feel **in**cluded rather than **ex**cluded.

10 I can *"touch hearts"* today if I compliment individuals.

11 *Let us pray:*

Loving Lord, inspire me
to bring out the best in others
and "touch hearts"
by being welcoming and generous
and always positive in attitude,
showing individuals
that they matter and are important.
May those
who are part of my life this day
treat me in the same way
as I treat them. Amen.

✍ See also 7 April. For "touching hearts" see also 3 February, 9 June, 10 July.

✍ The theologian Martin Buber has written: "Individuals wish to be confirmed in their being by another and wish to have a presence in the being of the other... secretly and bashfully watching for a 'YES' which allows that person to be - and which can only come from one person to another. It is from one person to another that the heavenly bread of self-being is passed."

✍ John Baptist De La Salle was born in Rheims, France, 30/4/1651. John was the first to dignify teaching as a ministry in itself. He is remembered as having built up communities of Brother-teachers who would be faithful and of support to each other, consecrated by vows; this was a new development in the Church. John is credited as having started a workable teacher-training system some 200 years before it was taken up elsewhere. He is also remembered for composing several inspirational books for teachers, and he advocated that a library should be at the disposal of students. He broke the long-standing practice of teaching members of a class one by one, developing the process of teaching a group of students simultaneously. In other schools pupils were taught first to read in Latin, but John revolutionised education by teaching through the language of the people - Latin being useless to the children of the poor. He is also remembered for having founded the first schools for delinquents, and the first secondary schools for modern languages, arts and the sciences, as well as technical schools which offered agricultural courses and pracical workshops. John died on 7/4/1719. He was canonised in 1900 and declared the Patron of Teachers in 1950 by Pope Pius XII. 25 De La Salle Brothers - all educators, and 20 of them martyrs - now join him in being called "Blessed" or "Saint". Some further details about John's life and inspiration can be obtained by writing to the author, or locating on the Internet: http://www.dlsnet.demon.co.uk or follow "Lasallian" in a web-search.

✍ Could include in the reflection (after paragraph 1): "John Baptist De La Salle encouraged people to spend a few quiet seconds every hour of the day, calling to mind that God is with them. Let's reflect in silence for a moment that we are in God's Presence, because Jesus said that when two or three gather together in his name then he would be with us..."

🎼 If I am lacking love; O let all who thirst; We come to you, Lord, teach us how to pray

1 One of the world's great painters, Vincent Van Gogh, was born in Holland in 1853. He lived briefly in England and Belgium, and then went to live in Paris with his brother, Theo, an art dealer, before moving to Arles in Provence, southern France.

2 He produced a drawing or a picture every day for the last few years of his life, but it's thought that he only sold one painting during his life-time, and he felt a failure as well as suffering from moods, depression, instability and even madness, cutting off part of his right ear.

3 He committed himself voluntarily to a mental asylum. There he continued to paint, and he produced a portrait of a doctor who helped him. That painting is called *"Portrait of Doctor Gachet"*, and it became the world's most expensive painting on this day in 1990 when it was sold at auction for £45.5 million.

4 *Let's pray in silence for a moment for all who are going through great difficulties...*

   (pause...)

5 *Let's pray in silence that we may be people who support and encourage others...*

   (pause ...)

6 *Let's think in silence for a moment of two people to set out to encourage today...*

   (pause...)

✍ *Van Gogh wrote:*
"I am rich because I have found in my work something to which I can devote myself heart and soul, and which gives meaning and significance to my life."

✍ *Sister Wendy Becket, the art critic, remarks that Van Gogh, like Rembrandt, had the rare power to take the ugly and make it beautiful through his paintings.*

✍ *Van Gogh wrote to his brother Theo:*
"I want to paint people with that something of the eternal which the halo symbolised, which I aim to convey by the radiance of my colouring."

✍ *Vincent Van Gogh: 30/3/1853-27/7/1890. He died, aged 37, from a self-inflicted gunshot wound. We know of about 750 paintings and 1600 drawings of his.*

✍ *Van Gogh's "Portrait of Doctor Gachet" sold within 3 minutes at auction at Christie's in New York. Bought by a Japanese businessman [Van Gogh himself had been influenced by Japanese painting], the portrait was put on sale again on 29/9/1997, and was sold for much less than was paid for it. Other paintings around that time also sold as a loss - the 1980s having been a "bubble" in the art market, when prices were greatly inflated.*

𝄞 In you, my God; Oh the love of my Lord
   ("all the beauty I see")

1 In 1863, the "Football Association" was founded, to set out clear rules for the game and to distinguish it from rugby football and other similar games. With the foundation of the Football Association, the game began to be called "association" or "**assoc**", giving the word "soccer", which at first was a slang word.

2 In May each year the Cup Final is held at Wembley. After the First World War it became a tradition for community singing to take place at the Football Cup Final at Wembley. King George V *(the fifth)* suggested that a hymn be included, and *"Abide with me"* was chosen. It is still sung before the Cup Final every May.

3 The words were written by Henry Lyte in the fishing village of Brixham in Devon, where he had been the vicar since the age of 30. His words are particularly touching because he wrote them whilst dying of T.B. - tuberculosis.

4 On the 4th September 1847 he said goodbye to the congregation of his church. He had been given early retirement because of his chronic health. In his last sermon he preached about the time when two disciples were walking along a road towards a village called Emmaus. Jesus had been killed a few days before, but now he joins them and walks beside them. He is risen from the dead. At last they recognise him and say to him: *"Stay with us. It is nearly evening."*

5 Henry Lyte took this theme and wrote his hymn as he walked by the sea. He heard the ebb and flow of the tide and, for the last time there, he watched the sun set. The following day he was to go abroad on the advice of his doctor, who had told him that in a drier climate he might live a little longer.

6 And so he wrote *"Abide with me"* (meaning "stay with me"), "it is fast becoming evening." As he wrote his words, Henry Lyte also thought of his own life coming to a swift end. No earthly helpers or comforts could make much difference to him.

7 2 months later, on his way to sunny Italy, he died in Nice, France. His last words were *"Peace, joy,"* as he pointed his hand towards the sky.

8 The words of his hymn we'll make our prayer today. We can use our imagination and place ourselves on the seashore as the sun is setting. We listen to the words of his hymn as the prayer of this sick man who knew he was at the "evening" of his life, about to die from tuberculosis - but at peace with himself:

9 **Abide with me,**
   fast falls the eventide;
the darkness deepens,
   Lord, with me abide.
When other helpers fail,
   and comforts flee,
help of the helpless,
   O abide with me.

10 **Swift to its close**
   ebbs out life's little day;
earth's joys grow dim,
   its glories pass away;
change and decay
   in all around I see;
O thou who changest not,
   abide with me.

11 **I need thy presence**
   every passing hour;
what but thy grace
   can foil the tempter's power?
Who like thyself
   my guide and stay can be?
Through cloud and sunshine,
   O abide with me.

12 I fear no foe with thee
      at hand to bless;
  ills have no weight
      and tears no bitterness.
  Where is death's sting?
      Where, grave, thy victory?
  I triumph still,
      if thou abide with me.

13 Hold thou thy Cross
      before my closing eyes;
  shine through the gloom,
      and point me to the skies;
  heaven's morning breaks,
      and earth's vain shadows flee:
  in life, in death,
      O Lord, abide with me.

🔊 See also 12 June re the banning of football.

🔊 "Emmaus" is pronounced "Im-ay-uss".

🔊 Parts of the first 2 verses are based on words
    at the end of St Luke's gospel, chapter 24. Two
    disciples were disillusioned because Jesus had
    been killed. As they walk along the road towards
    Emmaus, just outside Jerusalem, Jesus himself
    joins them and walks with them. At first they
    don't recognise him. "It is evening, and the day
    is almost over," they said to him. "Come and
    stay with us."

🔊 The words in the 4th verse - "Where is death's
    sting? Where, grave, thy victory?" - are a quote
    from St Paul: 1 Cor 15^{55}. This hymn is often
    chosen to be sung at funerals.

🔊 Henry Francis Lyte (1793-1847) also wrote the
    words of the hymn, "Praise my soul, the king
    of heaven".

🔊 Arthur Caiger had led community singing on
    Armistice Day, 11/11/1918, and he also led the
    community singing for the Cup Final, includ-
    ing songs that were sung during the war.

🔊 King George V was the grandfather of Queen
    Elizabeth II.

🔊 'Abide with me' was the favourite hymn of the
    Indian leader Ghandi, who was a Hindu. The
    hymn is still played on India's Republic Day,
    as the sun goes down.

(See also 14 March and 18 April.)

1 In 1905 the scientist, Albert Einstein, produced his *"Special Theory of Relativity"*, which linked time and space and movement.

2 A week ago, the 11th May, was the anniversary in 1916 of Einstein producing a new *"General Theory of Relativity"* about gravity and space.

3 Einstein was born a German and was of Jewish background. For many years there was hatred and rivalry between Germany and France, and he was all too well-aware of the persecution of the Jews down the ages. Einstein said:

4 *"If my Theory of Relativity*
is proven correct,
Germany will claim me as a German,
and France will declare
that I am a citizen of the world.
Should my theory prove untrue,
France will say that I am a German,
and Germany will declare that I am a Jew."

5 *Let us pray:*

Lord, I ask for the gifts
of knowledge and wisdom
and understanding.
What I pray for
I intend to work at,
so that I may be someone
with an open mind,
a thirst for knowledge,
and a wisdom that makes good use
of my knowledge and experience.
I know that any gifts are useless
if I do not also have
love and concern for others,
and so I ask that you inspire me
to live in such a way
that I am caring and compassionate
and promote understanding
between people.
May others respect me, Lord,
as much as I respect them. Amen.

✍ *Could use instead the prayers of 29 January or 21 March or 4 May. The last two lines of the prayer above could be used regularly in class.*

✍ *Einstein produced his "General Theory" in 1916, during the course of the First World War. He spoke these words at the Sorbonne, Paris, some years later in December 1929. Being a Jew, he decided to leave Germany in 1933 when Hitler came to power and the imprisonment of Jews began.*

♪ If I am lacking love; Oh the word of my Lord; There is a world

19 MAY

1 In Saint Paul's Cathedral in London, visitors can climb stairs so as to walk around the inside of the great dome, which is 60 metres (200 feet) across. This ledge (or balcony) is called the Whispering Gallery because the sound from someone's whisper bounces back from the smooth walls of the dome. Even someone whispering on the other side of the dome can be heard if people listen close to the wall.

2 It was whilst on this Whispering Gallery just over a hundred years ago that a poor shoemaker whispered to his girlfriend that he didn't have enough money to buy leather to make shoes, and so didn't have enough money for them to get married.

3 On the other side of the dome someone heard the whispering of the couple and decided he would help them. He followed the shoemaker from a distance to find out where he lived, and then he paid for some leather and arranged for it to be sent anonymously to the shoemaker's shop. Everything went well because the shoemaker was then able to make enough money from his shop, and so the couple were able to marry.

4 It was a few years later that they found out who it was who had helped them. It was the Prime Minister, William Gladstone, and today was the day of his death in 1898.

5 *Let us pray:*

Lord, most of us
will not become well-known
or be written about
because of great achievements,
but we will be known and loved
for our attitude
and the smaller ordinary things
that we do
that make our part of the world
a better place.
Inspire us, Lord, each day,
to find joy in giving
as well as in receiving,
and lead us to act justly,
love tenderly,
and walk humbly with you, our God.
Amen.

❖❖❖❖❖❖❖❖❖❖❖❖❖❖❖❖❖❖❖❖

✍ *The hymn "Whatsoever you do" - based on Mt 25 - could be adapted and recited as a prayer.*

✍ *Mt 25[31-40] - At the Last Judgement, those who are praised for doing good, genuinely ask: "But when was it **you** that we fed and gave drink to....?" 'Doing good' has become second-nature to them, as acting indifferently has become second-nature to the others who receive the consequences of **their** attitude and actions - Mt 25[41-46].*

✍ *Mt 6[1-4] - "Don't parade your good deeds before others, to attract their attention. When you give money to help others, your left hand mustn't know what your right hand is doing. Your Father, seeing all that is done in secret, will reward you."*

✍ *"There is more joy in giving than in receiving," said Jesus, as quoted in Acts 20[35]. "Act justly, love tenderly, walk humbly..." - Micah 6[8].*

✍ *William Ewart Gladstone: 29/12/1809-19/5/1898. He had four Administrations as Liberal Prime Minister: 1868-74, 1880-5, 1886, 1892-4. see also 13 September.*

🎼 If I am lacking love; Take my hands; Seek ye first

1 In the Church's Year, May has been called "the month of Mary". In our prayer we can think of the times that Jesus' Mother is mentioned in the Gospels as she supports her Son. We pray:

2 **Mary, chosen by God,**
you believed the angel's message
and became the Mother of Jesus.
You welcomed
shepherds and wise men:
> *Pray for us, Mary,*
> *that Jesus may live in us.*

3 **Mary, you were beside Jesus**
at the wedding feast at Cana,
and you noticed
that the servants were worried
that the wine was running out.
You told them to do
whatever Jesus would ask of them,
and then he changed
water into wine
in jars that the servants
had filled to the brim:
> *Mary, ask your Son*
> *to fill us with the Holy Spirit.*

4 **Mary, your love met Jesus, your Son,**
as he suffered on the cross:
> *Mary, in your love, support us*
> *as we carry our crosses*
> *in daily life.*

5 **Mary,**
you stayed with the friends of Jesus,
waiting for the Holy Spirit
to change their lives at Pentecost:
> *Mary, wait with us*
> *and our families and friends*
> *so that we, too,*
> *may receive all the promises*
> *of Jesus, your Son.*
> *Amen.*

📖 *Or, as a prayer, could recite the six verses of Damian Lundy's hymn, "Oh Mary, when our God chose you", which mentions Mary's place in key events.*

📖 *Or could use one of Bishop David Konstant's Rosary reflections that are part of his book, "Jesus Christ, the Way, the Truth and the Life" [Collins] 0-00-599681-3.*

📖 *Paragraph 2: Lk 1^{26-35}, Lk 2^{1-20}, Mt 2^{1-12}; paragraph 3: Jn 2^{1-11}; paragraph 4: Jn 19^{25-27}; paragraph 5: Acts 1^{12-14}.*

📖 *See also 15 August and 24 September*

🎵 As I kneel before you; Holy Virgin, by God's decree; Oh Mary, when our God chose you; The angel Gabriel

21 MAY

(See also 17 June)

1 We can look at the stars in the sky at night, and we might wonder about the significance and worth of a single person amidst the vastness of the Universe.

2 If an adult human body was analysed, we would discover that it is made of:

3 - about 45 litres of water;

4 - enough carbon to make the lead of 9,000 pencils;

5 - enough phosphorus for the heads of 2,000 matches;

6 - enough iron to make a nail;

7 - about 30 grams of other metals;

8 - enough fat to make about 8 bars of soap;

9 - enough sulphur to rid a dog of fleas;

10 - enough lime to whitewash a small shed.

11 Human beings, of course, are very much more than chemicals - we are individuals with feelings, talents, relationships, and a personal history.

12 *Let us pray:*

Lord God,
I can think of some of the chemicals
my body is made of
and the way
the different cells of my body interact,
but I know how much more
a human being really is.
I pray that I may always appreciate
the wonder
of the human body, mind and spirit.
I pray for good health,
an enquiring mind,
and a spirit that seeks all that is good,
knowing that I will only
be fully at rest and in peace
as I live in your presence. Amen.

🖾 *Or could use as a prayer Psalm 8 [see 12 April] or Psalm 138/139 [see 10 February].*

🖾 *Isaiah 43[4] - "You are precious in my eyes and I love you".*

🖾 *Shakespeare wrote:*

"What a piece of work is a man!
How noble in reason!
How infinite in faculty!
In form, in moving,
how express and admirable!
In action, how like an angel!...
The beauty of the world!
The paragon of animals!"
- *Hamlet, Act 2, Scene 2, 1.*

"Paragon" = the most perfect

🎵 Amazing grace; Christ be beside me; Come, come, follow me; Do not worry over what to eat; Happy the man; O Lord my God, when I in awesome wonder

1 Victor Hugo was one of the greatest French authors, and he died on this day in 1885. One of his most famous books has been made into a musical that has been performed across the world.

2 The book and the musical are called *"Les Misérables"*, telling of a thief - Jean Valjean - who is released from being chained in a floating prison for 19 years. His imprisonment has taken away his sense of living as a human being. On his release, no-one will help him because he is an ex-prisoner. Eventually a priest invites him to have a meal. Valjean leaves the house during the night, stealing what is valuable from the priest's house. Soldiers come upon him and arrest him as he acts suspiciously. They discover the valuables and take him back to the priest. Wanting to give him a break, a chance, the priest lies and says that he has given him the valuables.

3 Forgiven and treated generously, Valjean decides to change his life. He can only break with the past, he feels, if people no longer know that he is a former prisoner. He decides to take on a new name, and moves to a small town, where eventually he becomes mayor, and helps people.

4 Because Jean Valjean has broken the law in not reporting regularly to the police, a policeman (called Javert) searches for him, year after year. The policeman happens to arrive in the town where the ex-prisoner has become the mayor, but he does not recognise him. One day there is an accident and someone becomes trapped under a runaway cart. Immediately the mayor lifts one end of the heavy cart with his back. The policeman who sees this knows of only one other man with such strength - the prisoner he is looking for: Jean Valjean.

5 *'Les Misérables'* continues with love stories and escapes, telling of the courage and the struggle to improve the lives of all who are poor and deprived.

6 *'Les Misérables'* is one of the world's most popular musicals. The Finale includes these words:

*"To love another person
is to touch the face of God."*

7 The first part of our prayer is based on a prayer written by Victor Hugo, the author of *'Les Misérables'*:

8 *Let us pray:*

**We who weep come to you, Lord,
because you always
share our sorrow.
We who suffer come to you,
knowing that you cure.
We who are afraid come to you,
because you smile on us.
We share in your life
because you share ours
and so we know, God of love,
that "to love another person
is, indeed, to touch your face".
May we live in your love forever.
Amen.**

The words of the Finale:

*"To love another person
is to touch the face of God."*

📖 *An alternative prayer:*

**Lord, may people be as ready
    to give me a break, a chance,
    and let me make a new start,
    as I am ready
    to be generous to others.
Forgive me my faults
    in the same way
    as I forgive and accept other people.
Amen.**

📖 *In October 1995 in London's Royal Albert Hall, 250 actors from across the world came together for a 10th anniversary concert. The Finale featured 17 actors who had played the hero, Valjean, and each sang a line or two in his own language.*

📖 *An organisation that works with prisoners, former prisoners and their families, is: The Bourne Trust, 1-3 Brixton Rd., London SW9 6DE*

📖 *Similar to the words quoted from the Finale are these by the Roman philosopher, Seneca, who wrote shortly before his death in 65 AD: "No-one is so near God as the person who shows kindness." He was not a Christian.*

📖 *Victor Hugo (26/2/1802-22/5/1885) wrote to his publisher in 1862. As the author of 'Les Misérables', he wanted to know if the book was successful and selling. He simply wrote " ? ", to which his publisher replied: " ! " He wrote the book during his 15-year exile from France on the Channel Island of Guernsey. Hugo also wrote "The Hunchback of Notre Dame".*

🎼 Father, I place into your hands; If I am lacking love; In you, my God; Oh the love of my Lord

1 We bring before the Lord
those who have recently
been baptised or confirmed
- or who are about to be -
that they may be true to themselves
and may live their faith
in a genuine and credible way.
Lord, in your mercy,
hear our prayer.

2 We pray for our families and friends
that the power of the Holy Spirit
may be in our lives,
so that we may live fully with his gifts
of wisdom and understanding,
of knowledge and right judgement,
of courage and reverence,
and of wonder and awe
in God's presence.
Lord, in your mercy,
hear our prayer.

3 Let's pray for those about to sit exams,
that nothing may prevent them
from doing as well as they deserve.
Lord, in your mercy,
hear our prayer.

4 We pray for all in the mass media
- in TV, radio, films,
newspapers, advertising
and the Internet,
that they may be guided
by good principles
and the best motives.
We pray for wisdom ourselves
that, amidst the influences
and pressures around us,
we may make good decisions
and grow in wisdom and character
each day.
Lord, in your mercy,
hear our prayer.

1 An old Chinese story tells of a farmer whose only horse runs away. "How terrible!" say his neighbours. "Maybe!" says the farmer.

2 The next day his horse returns, bringing along three wild horses. "How wonderful!" say his neighbours. "Maybe!" says the father.

3 The following day his son tries to tame one of the wild horses, but he falls off and breaks his leg. "How terrible!" say his neighbours. "Maybe!" says the farmer.

4 The next day some soldiers come along to force young men of the village to join them in war. Because the lad has a broken leg, he is left behind. "How fortunate!" say the neighbours. "Maybe!" says the farmer.

5 The soldiers, still one man short, take the young man's cousin instead. "How dreadful!" say the farmer's neighbours. "Maybe!" says the farmer.

6 That night a landslide covers the house in which the cousin would have been sleeping if he had not been taken by the soldiers. "How fortunate!" say the friends. "Maybe!" says the farmer.

7 And so the story could go on! One of life's great lessons is this: we're never sure just how things are going to turn out. We'll live a good life if our attitude is always positive - determined to make the best of **all** situations that come our way.

8 *Let us pray:*

**Lord Jesus, you promised
to be with your people always,
and so we know that you are with us
in good times and bad.
Nothing that ever happens to us
can separate us from your love.
Help us always to be positive
in our attitude
that we may seek and find
the best in people and in situations,
and so draw good
out of all that happens to us.
Amen.**

📖 See also *25 May for similar ideas. Is my attitude, for instance, to see that a bottle is half-full, or do I see it as half-empty?*

📖 *Romans 8$^{35-39}$ - nothing can separate us from God's love. - See 29 June.*

📖 *In his "De Profundis", Oscar Wilde writes:* "Where there is sorrow, there is holy ground."

📖 *Rabbi Harold Kushner reflects on always seeking to make the best of situations in his book, "When Bad Things Happen to Good People", Pan Books, 0-330-26827-9.*

🎵 Come, come, follow me; Do not worry over what to eat; Father, I place into your hands; Follow me; For to those who love God

1 Major problems occurred during the Apollo 13 Space Mission to the Moon in 1970, but the men returned safely.

2 Jim Lovell was the Commander of Apollo 13, and he once talked of piloting an aeroplane in combat conditions. He was to fly back and land on his aircraft carrier, but his radar and homing signal had failed. A great ocean lay before him, he was fast running out of fuel, and he was too far out to sea to return to the land. Where was the aircraft carrier? In which direction should he fly?

3 He thought that matters couldn't get worse, and then, suddenly, all his cockpit lights went out. Then, below him, as his eyes became adjusted to the darkness, he could see a long path of green phosphorescent algae. There could only be one explanation for that long path - the aircraft carrier must have churned up the algae in the sea. All he had to do, with his fuel running low, was to fly along that phosphorescent path, and then he would be able to land on the aircraft carrier.

4 *"I thought it a disaster"* he said *"that the lights in my aircraft went out, but if they had not gone out, I would never have been able to see the algae which led me back to the ship, and I would have died in the sea when my fuel ran out. Some things work out well when you least expect them to."*

5 *Let us pray for God's protection, using a prayer of St Columba, written 1400 years ago:*

Be a bright flame before me, Lord.
Be a guiding star above me.
Be a smooth path below me.
Be a kindly shepherd behind me
- today, tonight, and forever. Amen.

✍ *Tom Hanks played the role of Jim Lovell in the film, "Apollo 13", relaeased in 1995.*

✍ *See also 24 May. Could use the prayer for 10 May or 24 May.*

✍ *St Columba of Iona: about 521-597*

🎶 Amazing grace; Be still and know I am with you; Christ be beside me; For to those who love God; I am with you forever; I will be with you; Yahweh, I know you are near

26 MAY

1   We're going to listen to three one-sentence quotes:

2   The American poet, Walt Whitman, who died on this day in 1892, said:
    *"In the faces of men and women
    I see God."*

3   The musical of *'Les Misérables'* has these words in its Finale:
    *"To love another person
    is to touch the face of God."*

4   A Church document says that
    *"The human person
    is the clearest reflection
    of God among us."*

5   *Let us pray:*

    **Father, God of love,
    as I come to recognise you
    in the faces of those people
    you have placed into my life,
    I ask that I may grow
    as the loving person
    you call me to be. Amen.**

📖 *An alternative prayer could be:*
> Grant me to recognise in others,
> Lord God,
> the radiance of your own face. Amen.

📖 *Could make use of the Grail Prayer* ["Lord Jesus, I give you my hands"], *or* "Christ has no body on earth now but ours" - *both of which are to be found on 28 March.*

📖 *Walt Whitman: 31/5/1819-26/5/1892.*

📖 *See 22 May for Victor Hugo's 'Les Misérables'. See also the quote from 22 May.*

📖 *"The human person" quote is from 'The Common Good',[12], by the Bishops of England and Wales.*

📖 *Gerard Manley Hopkins writes:*
> "Christ plays in ten thousand places,
> lovely in limbs,
> and lovely in eyes not his
> To the Father
> through the features of men's faces."
> *- from 'As Kingfishers Catch Fire'.*

📖 *2 Cor 3^{18} ,4^{5-6} - The Father's glory is reflected in the face of Jesus.*

🎵 If God is for us; If I am lacking love; Lay your hands

1 1,400 years ago a monk called Gregory saw some boys being sold as slaves in Rome. They looked alike with fair hair and blue eyes, and Gregory asked where they were from. *"They are Angles,"* he was told. *"Angles?"* Gregory replied; *"They look like angels!"*

2 When Gregory became Pope, he sent a group of 30 monks from Rome to bring the Gospel to the Angles and Saxons in what we now know as England. Leading the group was Augustine. As they travelled through Gaul (France) the group began to lose heart as they heard how rough it would be to cross the English Channel, and particularly how fierce the occupants of the country were reported to be.

3 Augustine returned to Rome, but Pope Gregory the Great sent him back with encouraging words for the whole group. In the year 597 they landed on the Kent coast. They discovered that the wife of the King of Kent was already a Christian, and the monks were well-received. Augustine - sometimes called Austin - became the first Archbishop of Canterbury, and many people became Christians.

4 The ancient Britons - whose land and country had been taken over by the Angles and Saxons - understandably were hesitant to trust any newcomers, even fellow-Christians. Augustine's attempts to reconcile fellow-Christians about Church matters were not successful, and there were mistakes made on both sides.

5 St Augustine of Canterbury is known as the *'Apostle of the English'.* Today, 27th May, is his feastday. Two days later in 1982, the Anglican Archbishop of Canterbury spoke to the Pope during John-Paul's visit to Canterbury Cathedral, saying:

6 *"Augustine became the first Archbishop of Canterbury, and I rejoice that the successors of Pope Gregory and Archbishop Augustine stand here today in the church which is built on their partnership in the Gospel."*

7 *Let us pray:*

God our Father,
when times are difficult,
I ask for courage and determination.
When there is hostility between people,
lead me to see the best
in people and in situations,
and give me the gift of making peace.
Remove from me
whatever contradicts your love
that I may share more fully
the Good News of your love. Amen.

❧ *Alternative prayers could be those of 18 January, 8 February, 5 May.*

❧ *"Not angles but angels," said Gregory, and continued his play on words. "What region are they from?" "From Deira" [Yorkshire]. "Then they must be rescued from 'dei ira' - 'the wrath of God.'" "Who is their ruler?" "Aella." "Then 'Alleluia' must be sung in their land!"*

❧ *Different dates for Easter, and a different way of administering the Sacrament of Baptism were two of the differences in custom between the 'British' [Celtic] church - already established in the country - and the 'English church' that Augustine was introducing.*

❧ *Augustine is known as "the Apostle of the English" - as distinct from the 'British' - because many of the original inhabitants of the country, as mentioned, were already Christian, and the country's first martyr, St Alban, met his death in Roman Britain about the year 304AD, nearly 300 years before Augustine's arrival [see 20 June for details].*

❧ *Just before Augustine started his ministry [landing in the year 597], St Columba from Ireland began missionary work that spread throughout Scotland, founding his monastery on the island of Iona on the west coast in 563. A set of four British philatelic stamps were issued in 1997, commemorating the 1400th anniversary of the death of St Columba, and the 1400th anniversary of the arrival of St Augustine.*

❧ *Bede's 'A History of the English Church and People' tells of the events mentioned here. See also the CTS booklet "Augustine of Canterbury, 14th Centenary, 597-1997" by Edwin Bannon, FSC, 1-86082-009-3*

🎵 Come, come, follow me; Follow me; God's Spirit is in my heart; He who would valiant be

MAY 28

1 On this day in 1982 Pope John Paul II started his Visit to Great Britain. Later in the day he met many sick and disabled people and gave them the Sacrament of the Sick. Only a year after being shot and seriously wounded, he spoke to those who were ill or disabled:

2 *"I myself have had a share in suffering, and I have known the physical weakness that comes with injury and sickness. It is precisely because I have experienced suffering that I am able to affirm with ever-greater conviction that nothing at all can ever separate us from the love of God.*

3 *"Dear friends, there is no force or power that can block God's love for you. Sickness and suffering seem to contradict all that is worthy, all that is desired. And yet no disease, no injury, no infirmity can ever deprive you of your dignity as children of God.*

4 *"We often find in the Gospels the loving bond of affection between Jesus and the sick or disabled. We believe in Christ's healing love, and we reaffirm that nothing will separate us from that love. Surely Jesus wishes to say: 'Be clean; be healed; be strong; be saved.' "*

5 *Let us pray:*

Lord Jesus, we read in the gospel
  that you spoke individually
  to many people and said:
"Be cured";   *Lk 5¹³*
"Get up and walk";   *Lk 5²⁴*
"What do you want me to do for you?"
                        Mt 20³²
"Of course I want to cure you: be healed";
                        Mt 8³
"Let what you want be done for you";
                        Mt 9²⁹
"Receive your sight";   *Lk 18⁴²*
"Receive back your hearing"; *Mk 7³⁴*
"Young man, arise";   *Lk 7¹⁵*

"Go, your son will live";   *Jn 4⁵⁰*
"Go, your faith has saved you." *Mk 10⁵²*
Knowing that you are present
  in our midst,
we ask you today
to touch each one of us individually
and bring us your healing
of body, mind and spirit. Amen.

📖 *See also 13 May and the quote and prayer of 11 February.*

📖 *Paragraphs 2 & 3 were spoken by the Pope in Southwark Cathedral, London, 28/5/82. Paragraph 4 is taken from the Pope's address to the handicapped and their carers in Edinburgh, 1/6/82.*

📖 *In Southwark Cathedral Pope John Paul also said:* "You will find the crucified Lord in the midst of your sickness and suffering."

📖 *James 5¹⁴⁻¹⁵ - If anyone is ill, call for the church elders and have the person prayed over and anointed with oil in the name of Jesus.*

🎵 Be not afraid; Do not be afraid; I heard the Lord call my name; In you, my God; Lay your hands

51

29 MAY

1. Mount Everest is part of the Himalayas mountain range in south-east Asia, on the frontier of Nepal and Tibet. It is the highest peak in the world - over 8,800 metres (over 29,000 feet) above sea level.

2. After many unsuccessful and sometimes fatal attempts to reach the top, Mount Everest was finally "conquered" on this day in 1953 by two members of a British expedition - Edmund Hillary from New Zealand, and Tenzing Norkay, a local guide from Nepal. They stayed at the summit for only 15 minutes, and there planted the flags of Britain, Nepal, India, and the United Nations.

3. This was a very great achievement. No-one we know is likely to achieve so much, but each of us has *"Mount Everests"* in our own lives - various difficulties that need effort and maybe team work to conquer.

4. We can think, too, that a walk of 20 metres for a person with a physical disability or serious illness may be one of the greatest achievements of that individual's life. Such a short walk would be taken for granted by most people. What one person may achieve with very little effort may be a **great** achievement for someone with different abilities.

5. What really counts is the effort we put into something to make it our own best. My *"success"* and *"achievement"* can only be measured against my own potential.

6. *Let us pray:*

   Lord, I ask that you inspire me
   always to do my best
   - not comparing myself with others,
   but only with myself.
   Lead me, Lord,
   to discover and use
   my own talents to the full.

May I live in such a way
that I help others
to experience success.
Inspire me to be generous
in praising others
for the good use of their abilities
- looking not so much
at the degree of achievement
but at the effort put in. Amen.

📖 George Leigh Mallory, on being asked why he wanted to climb Mount Everest, replied: "Because it's there!" He died in an attempted climb in 1924.

📖 The leader of the successful 1953 expedition, Sir John Hunt, wrote: "The greatness of climbing on the highest hills lies in the fact that no single man is capable of reaching the summit by his own efforts."

📖 The news that Mount Everest had been conquered was delayed being broadcast so as not to 'eclipse' the Coronation of the 27-year old Queen Elizabeth II. News of Everest reached Britain 4 days after reaching the summit, on the day of the Coronation itself - 2nd June 1953.

📖 See also 24 August.

📖 Some of our brothers and sisters have "Mount Everests" in their lives because of disability, a change of circumstances, different abilities, chronic illness, trauma, feeling inadequate, etc.

🎵 Christ be beside me; Do not worry *("go do your best today")*; Father in my life I see; I am with you forever; I watch the sunrise; Thank you for fathers; Walk with me, O my Lord *("the steepest mountainside")*; Yahweh, I know you are near *("if I climb to the heavens")*

1 On his Visit to Britain in 1982, Pope John Paul II spoke in Glasgow. The Pope said that Jesus offers a new way of living:

2 *"to be gentle, generous, simple,*
and above all, sincere;
to avoid being arrogant,
fault-finding, or self-seeking.
The disciples of the new Kingdom
must seek happiness
even amidst poverty, deprivation,
tears and oppression.
To aim for the Kingdom
requires a radical change
in outlook, in mentality, in behaviour,
in relationships with others.

3 *Jesus offers a new way of life...*
He has a specific task in life
for each and every one of us.
Each of us is hand-picked,
called by name by Jesus."

4 Let us pray:

Lord Jesus,
   you call us friends
   and you call each one of us
   by name.
May your Holy Spirit
   be fully alive in us
   that we may truly
   appreciate and love ourselves,
   and so more readily
   value and serve others.
When we experience sorrow
   or the loss of someone,
   give us courage and support
   that we may better encourage others
   who share
   the same kind of experience.
Lead us to act justly and fairly,
   helping people
   to see the best in one another,
   so that those who have fallen out
   may be reconciled and live in peace.

May we learn always
   to be genuine and sincere,
   avoiding arrogance
   and doing others down,
   treating other people
   as the equals that they are.
Bless us when times are hard,
   and walk with us
   as the Good Shepherd
   who leads and protects. Amen.

✍ *Pope John Paul's words were spoken at a Mass in Bellahouston Park in Glasgow, 1/6/82.*

✍ *"You call us friends" - Jn 15[14]. After the first two paragraphs the prayer is based loosely on the Beatitudes in Mt 5[1-12]. Encouraging others who go through the same kind of difficulty - cf 2 Cor 1[2].*

✍ *"Love your neighbour **as** you love **yourself.**" - found in Lk 10[27], quoting from the Old Testament: Lev 19[18].*

♪ Be not afraid; Come, come, follow me; Do not be afraid; Do not worry; Follow me; I heard the Lord call my name; Oh Lord all the world belongs to you

31 MAY

1 In the 1980s, the Headteacher of a school in Boston in the United States wrote a letter to new teachers who joined the school each year. In her letter, she mentioned that she is a victim of a Nazi concentration camp. There she saw how some people had mis-used the good education they had received:

2 - highly-qualified engineers had built gas chambers;

3 - educated doctors experimented on children;

4 - trained nurses killed babies;

5 - some of those who did well at school and university then gassed men, women and children, and burned their bodies in huge ovens.

6 This headteacher said that she is suspicious of education because she has seen some highly-educated people behave in a most inhumane way. In her letter to new teachers she reminds them that **real education is to make young people more human.**

7 During the Second World War, Adolf Eichmann had been in charge of what was called *"The Final Solution"* of the Jews - the murder of all Jews throughout Europe. Eichmann escaped from Germany at the end of the War, and hid in Argentina until Israeli agents captured him in 1960 and took him to Israel. There he was placed on trial. Many people commented on how ordinary a person he looked - they had thought he would somehow look evil. He denied responsibility for what he had done, saying that he was only following orders. He was convicted of *"Crimes against Humanity"*, and was executed two days later on this day, 31st May, in 1962.

8 *Let us pray:*

God our Father,
   I pray that I may live in such a way
   that I choose wisely each day,
   and take responsibility
   for the choices that I make.
Inspire me to use for good
   my education
   and all the challenges
   that I will face,
   that I may grow more fully human,
   and do good to those around me.
Teach me to discern good from evil
   that I may grow
   in integrity of character
   and develop a true sense of values
   through following Jesus,
   your Son and our Brother. Amen.

> Real education
> is to make people
> more human.

❖❖❖❖❖❖❖❖❖❖❖❖❖❖❖❖❖❖❖❖

 *During his Visit to Britain, Pope John Paul II said:*

"Education is the completion of the person. To be educated is to be more fitted for life; to have a greater capacity for appreciating what life is, what it has to offer, and what the person has to offer in return to the wider society...

(Education offers) something of lasting value to our students, an antidote to often immediate prospects of frustration and boredom, not to mention the uncertainty of the long-term future."

(This was part of an address to teachers and students at St Andrew's Teacher-Training College, Bearsden, near Glasgow, 1/6/82.)

All that I am; If I am lacking love; My Lord, my Master; Seek ye first; Take my hands

1 Helen Keller was born in the southern United States. When she was only 19 months old, a severe illness left her deaf and blind. It was extremely difficult for Helen and her family to communicate. As Helen could not hear anyone's voice to copy, she had not learned to speak. It was impossible to educate her until a young teacher called Annie Sullivan arrived. One of Annie's strengths, as she described it herself, was that she had been blind, and eventually she managed to "reach" Helen and was able to teach her.

2 Helen Keller graduated from college with honours, and later visited many countries, speaking about winning through, despite difficulties and physical handicaps. She died on this day in 1968.

3 Helen Keller said:
"Most of us take life for granted.
Only the deaf appreciate hearing;
only the blind realise
the manifold blessings that lie in sight.
It is the same old story
of not being grateful for what we have
until we lose it;
of not being conscious of health
until we are ill.
But I, who am blind,
can give one hint to those who see:
use your eyes
as if tomorrow you would be stricken.

4 *And the same method can be applied*
to the other senses:
hear the music of voices -
the song of the bird,
the mighty strains of an orchestra
- as if you would be stricken deaf tomorrow.

5 *Touch each object you want to touch*
as if tomorrow
your tactile sense would fail.
Smell the perfume of flowers,

taste with relish each morsel,
as if tomorrow
you would never smell and taste again.

6 *Make every sense glory*
in the pleasure and beauty
which the world reveals.
*Thus, at last, you will **really see**,*
and a new world of beauty
will open up before you.

7 *Let us pray:*

Lord our God, open us up to your Spirit
living within us,
that we may live fully
each day of our lives.
Touch us,
that we may become more aware
of all that is around us,
growing in a sense
of wonder and awe,
and in appreciation
for all that we see and hear
and touch, taste and smell.
May we live in such a way
that we never take anything
for granted,
but always be appreciative
and express our thanks
to those who are part of our lives.
Amen.

✿❖✿❖✿❖✿❖✿❖✿❖✿❖✿❖

✍ "tactile" - using the sense of touch.

✍ See also 3rd June, 1st September, and the prayer of 16 September.

✍ D.H.Lawrence wrote: "The sense of wonder - that is the sixth sense, and it is the natural religious sense" (from an essay: "Hymns in a Man's Life").

♪ Amazing grace; Christ is our king; Thank you for giving me the morning; Walk with me, O my Lord

2 JUNE

1 When a football match or another sports match is held between two local teams, it is called a "derby". How did we get the name?

2 In 1780, Edward Stanley, the 12th Earl of Derby, decided to have a bet with his neighbour. There would be a race of just their two horses. First of all they tossed a coin to decide what they should call the race; whoever won the toss would have the race called by his name.

3 Every year since then "the Derby" has been held, and it is the most famous of horse races held on the flat. It is usually run on the first Wednesday of every June, and has been held on the Epsom Downs in Surrey for over 200 years. Only three-year old horses can run in the Derby, and so no horse can ever win twice, although jockeys and owners can.

4 That first Derby was a competition between two neighbours, and so we often refer to a sports match between two local teams as a "derby".

5 That first Derby in 1780 was literally a "two horse race", giving us a phrase that we sometimes use in speech. If there are a few people in a competition - but only two strong runners - we might say "it's a two horse race".

6 *Let us pray:*

**Lord, you have given skills and talents
   to each of us,
   and you are pleased
   when we use them well.
I ask
   that I may work well with others
   and bring out the best in them
   as well as in myself.
Lead me to live in such a way
   that I show appreciation
   for the achievements
   of all who use their talents well.
Amen.**

🖎 *The original competition was between Lord Derby and his neighbour, Sir Charles Bunbury's horse, Diomid, won the two-horse race, but Lord Derby won the toss for the race to be named after him! Another race, "the Oaks", run two days after the Derby, is named after an estate of Lord Derby near Epsom. There are other horse races that now bear the same name e.g. the Kentucky Derby in the United States.*

🖎 *In the Derby of 4th June 1914, a Suffragette purposely ran on to the racecourse in front of the King's horse, and was killed (see also 14 June).*

🖎 *For a trial period in the 1990s the Derby has been held on a Saturday.*

JUNE 3

(See also 1st June and 1st September)

1 Helen Keller was blind and deaf. Only when she was aged six did she learn to speak. Slowly, with the help of others, she transformed what was negative in her life, and lived more fully than many people. Helen Keller said: .

2 *"I thank God for my handicaps*
   because, through them,
   I have found myself,
   my work, and my God."

3 *Let us pray:*

Lord our God,
   you have made me
   in your own likeness
   and you love all that you have made.
I thank you
   for all that has been positive
   in my life.
I ask that I may live in such a way
   that I may learn
   from whatever I may find
   is negative or hurtful in my life.
May my disabilities and weaknesses
   teach me
   how to be sensitive to individuals,
   that I may grow
   more caring and compassionate
   with others who experience difficulties.
May I grow in strength of character
   through all that happens to me,
   living fully each day.
Amen.

"I thank God for my handicaps
because, through them,
I have found myself,
my work, and my God."

📖 *Helen Keller: 1880-1968. She wrote:* "The greatest calamity that could befall a person is to have sight and yet fail to see."

🎵 Amazing grace; Christ is our king, let the whole world rejoice; Make me a channel of your peace; Walk with me, O my Lord

4 JUNE

1 Early in the Second World War, in May and June 1940, the German Army made great advances and kept pushing the British Expeditionary Force towards the sea, as well as the French and the Belgians. For a while, Hitler halted his advance outside the French port of Dunkirk. The Allied soldiers presumed they would all soon be captured as prisoners of war, and they destroyed much of their fighting equipment, to prevent the Germans using it.

2 Ships, small fishing boats and pleasure craft set out from England to try to rescue some of the many soldiers trapped around Dunkirk. By June 4th 1940, almost by a miracle, over 330,000 British, French and Belgium troops had been evacuated from Dunkirk, under gunfire from the Germans. Would Hitler now invade Britain?

3 On that same day, Winston Churchill, Britain's Prime Minister, gave one of his most famous speeches in the House of Commons:

4 *"We shall not flag or fail.*
We shall fight in France,
we shall fight on the seas and oceans,
we shall fight with growing confidence
and growing strength in the air.
We shall defend our island,
whatever the cost may be.
We shall fight on the beaches,
we shall fight on the landing grounds,
we shall fight in the fields and in the streets,
we shall fight in the hills;
we shall never surrender."

5 We'll use as our prayer some words of Saint Ignatius Loyola:

Teach us, good Lord,
to serve you as you deserve;
to give and not to count the cost;
to fight and not to heed the wounds;
to toil and not to seek for rest;
to labour and to ask for no reward,
save that of knowing
that we do your will. Amen.

6 Dunkirk was a terrible and humiliating defeat for Britain and her allies, but most of the men were rescued. Four years and two days afterwards, Britain and her allies would return on D-Day to start to liberate the occupied countries of Europe.

✍ *We are not certain why Hitler halted for a few days his advance outside Dunkirk. It may have been that he thought that Britain would ask for a peaceful settlement in those desperate days.*

✍ *The french spelling for the name of the town is "Dunkerque".*

𝄞 Come let us go up to the Lord

58

1 Whilst his brother, John F Kennedy, was President of the United States, Robert Kennedy became Attorney-General, the government chief law officer. One of the great problems of the time was prejudice and discrimination against people who were not white. Robert Kennedy and his brother (the President) had worked together with Martin Luther King (a black leader) to get Civil Rights laws passed by the United States Congress and Senate.

2 Both President John Kennedy and Martin Luther King were assassinated. On this day in 1968, Robert Kennedy was shot as he was campaigning to become President himself. He died the following day, aged 42. His murder depressed the hopes of many people.

3 Two months before his own death, Robert Kennedy spoke the following words after the assassination of Martin Luther King:

4 *"What we need... is not division.*
What we need... is not hatred.
What we need...
is not violence and lawlessness,
but love and wisdom and compassion
toward one another,
and a feeling of justice
toward those who still suffer..."

5 *Let us pray, using words based on that speech of Robert Kennedy:*

Lord, we pray
   that we may not be people
   of hatred or violence or lawlessness,
   but people of love and wisdom
   and compassion towards one another,
   having a sense of justice
   towards all who suffer.
These things that we pray for
   give us your grace to work for.
Amen.

📖 *Robert F. Kennedy: 1925-1968.*
He often concluded his speeches with this quote from the poet, George Bernard Shaw:
   'You see things as they are
   and you ask, "Why?"
   But I dream things that never were
   and I ask, "Why not?"'
Realising he often ended his speeches with this quote, as soon as he started these words journalists would rush out to be the first to phone their newspapers.

📖 *"Prejudice" - "pre-judging" - is the attitude; "discrimination" is the action.*

📖 *The last two lines of the prayer are words of Saint Thomas More.*

♪ All that I am...dream; If I am lacking love; Only a shadow...dream; Thank you for fathers [v.4]; There is a world

6 JUNE

1 In 1944, after nearly five years of war, British and Commonwealth troops and American troops were ready to cross from England to mainland Europe to start to free those countries occupied by the Nazis.

2 Where would the Allies land? Would they cross the Channel by the shortest route, to land near Calais? Would they land first on the British territory of Jersey and the other Channel islands, already occupied by the Germans? Yet both these places were the most heavily fortified and defended.

3 It was decided instead to land in Normandy, hoping that they would not be detected on their long journey across the sea - at least 150km (95 miles). On 6th June 1944 the D-Day landing took place in Normandy, involving hundreds of thousands of people working together. D-Day was a turning-point because it saw the start of the defeat of Hitler.

4 *Let us pray:*

Lord our God,
  inspire us to make our choices well
  and understand our responsibilities
  and the consequences of what we do.
Help us to make good use
  of the opportunities that come to us.
Lead us to be positive in our attitude,
  that we may work well with others
  and live this day to the full. Amen.

The Allied armies would have great difficulty landing, wherever they chose. Having decided upon Normandy, they wanted to know more details of the beaches and surrounding areas. The British government asked the public to send in any holiday photographs that they had but, obviously not wanting to let the Germans know where they were going to land, they asked for photos of much of the coastline of mainland Europe!

Hitler was convinced that Britain would first want to re-take the only British land to be occupied by the Germans - the Channel Islands. When the Germans first landed there in July 1940, a few thought they were on the Isle of Wight (being an island in the Channel), close to the British mainland. Hitler was so convinced that Britain would re-take the Channel Islands that, incredibly, a quarter of all the 'Atlantic Wall' defences were on those islands - many still remaining there today.

132,000 men were landed on D-Day. Within 3 weeks more than a million men had landed. On the 50th Anniversary, Queen Elizabeth II stood on one of the landing sites and said: "Veterans of the Normandy Campaign: you deserve your nations' thanks. May we, your fellow countrymen, be worthy of what you did for us."

*The term "D-Day" is used by military people, indicating the day on which activity is to take place. "D-minus two" is an easy way of referring to the day that is two days before the main action starts. "D", therefore, stands for "Day"- meaning **the** Day.*

Come let us go up to the Lord; This day God gives me; This is the day

1 King Robert the Bruce of Scotland had been defeated in battle and was pursued by his enemies. He hid in a cave and thought over his defeat and his difficulties. He had little hope left, and thought he should give up the struggle.

2 At that moment he saw a spider dangling by a long thread. It was trying to climb back up to its web, but kept falling back. The spider persevered and eventually succeeded in what it had set out to do.

3 King Robert the Bruce often told this story to remind others of the lesson he learned from the spider - to "stick with it" even though there are setbacks. He died on this day in 1329.

4 *Let us pray:*

Lord,
show me how to learn from others,
how to be patient,
and how to persevere. Amen.

On 24 June in 1314 King Robert the Bruce defeated the English army under King Edward II. The battle was fought at Bannockburn near Stirling in Scotland. England's army of some 25,000 men was defeated by the Scottish army of about a third of that number. The Battle of Bannockburn is mentioned at the end of Mel Gibson's film, "Braveheart". The battle is also alluded to in the very tuneful Scottish anthem, "Flower of Scotland".

Abide with me; Be not afraid; Be still and know I am with you; Do not be afraid

1 In March or April each year the Jewish community celebrates the Feast of Passover, calling to mind how God used Moses to lead the people from slavery in Egypt. 50 days later - in May or June - is held the Jewish Feast of Pentecost (from a Greek word for 50). It calls to mind that God gave the 10 Commandments to Moses.

2 The 10 Commandments can be phrased in this way:

1 *Give God the first place in your life.*

2 *Don't love anything more than you love God.*

3 *Show respect to everything that's holy, particularly God's name.*

4 *You need one day of the week free for rest and for worshipping God.*

5 *Respect your parents and all who care for you.*

6 *Do not kill anyone.*

7 *Sexual love is special - keep it for the person you're married to.*

8 *Don't take what isn't yours.*

9 *Don't do people down by spreading lies about them.*

10 *Don't be jealous of what others have.*

3 The 10 Commandments reflect a basic common-sense way of living. They can guide us in the short-term and long-term choices that we need to make for a good and happy life.

4 We'll use as a reflection today the words of a hymn that the Jewish community uses at the Feast of Pentecost:

5 **If all the ocean was ink,**
and if every blade of grass
was a quill with which to write;
if the earth itself was parchment,
and if every person
started to write on it,
there would not be enough ink or pens
or parchment or people
to write fully
of God's love and greatness.

🖎 *Pentecost - or 'Shavuot' in Hebrew - is some times called the Feast of Weeks (being 7 week - 50 days - after the Feast of Passover). The synagogue is decorated with flowers and frui as a reminder that, before the Temple in Jeru salem was destroyed nearly 2,000 years ago the Jews would take offerings of fruit to offei to God there. After the prayer service in the synagogue, the people go home to celebrate festival meal. Included in the meal are twe round loaves of bread which are both decorated with a ladder pattern as a reminder that Mo ses 'climbed' the mountain to receive the 10 Commandments.*

🖎 *The 10 Commandments can be found in Exo dus 20 and also Deuteronomy 5.*

🖎 *We could think of what 'rules' a large group might decide upon after a few weeks of bein stranded on a very remote desert island. The 10 Commandments have been likened to word on the package of something we have bought "This will last a long time and work well the maker's instructions are followed."*

🖎 *See 15 January for the particular "10 Com mandments" signed as a pledge by member. of the non-violent movement in the USA in 1963, campaigning for Civil Rights for non whites.*

🖎 *It was on the Jewish Feast of Pentecost tha the Holy Spirit came upon the Apostles (Act 2[1-12]). The Jewish Feast of Pentecost is 50 day after Passover; the Christian Feast of Pente cost (or 'Whit Sunday') is 50 days after Easte See 'Moveable Feasts' in this volume.*

🎼 O Lord, all the world belongs to you

(See also 10 June.)

1 One of England's greatest authors, Charles Dickens, died on this day in 1870.

2 He had started school at the age of 9 but had to leave when his father was imprisoned for debt. Charles Dickens was then aged 12 and he had to get a job to support himself. He found work in a shoe-polish factory, but felt humiliated and not in control of his own life. This experience would haunt him for the rest of his life. Later he would write a book called '**David Copperfield**', which reflected his own difficult experiences as a child.

3 Dickens used some of his novels to point out that many people suffered greatly at that time in Victorian England. These stories were a good way of encouraging people to look at how they might help make their part of the world a better place.

4 His stories were printed as a serial in a London newspaper. Dickens was in great demand as a public reader of his novels, which he tended to act out as he spoke.

5 Charles Dickens died in 1870. Queen Victoria wrote of him in her diary: "He is a very great loss. He had a large loving mind, and the strongest sympathy with the poor." He was buried in Westminster Abbey beside the graves of the nation's kings and queens and other famous people.

6 We can reflect on some words written by Charles Dickens:

"Some great people
make others feel small,
but the real great people
are those who make others feel great."

7 Let's pause in silence to think just how I might help someone today to "feel great" about themselves.
(pause...)

8 Let us pray:

**Lord our God,
may I learn
to treat others generously,
with respect,
and with care and understanding,
that we may all
bring out the best in one another.
Amen.**

✎ The quote has been adapted to inclusive language.

✎ His first novel was called '**Pickwick Papers'**. Instead of being produced as a book, it was printed in chapters, month by month, and cost little to the many people who wanted to buy it.

✎ Some of his other books were: '**Oliver Twist**', '**A Christmas Carol**', '**Nicholas Nickleby**', '**Great Expectations**', '**Bleak House**', '**Little Dorritt**', '**The Old Curiosity Shop**', '**Hard Times**', and '**A Tale of Two Cities**'.

✎ Charles Dickens: 7/2/1812 - 9/6/1870. His image was shown on the back of the £10 note issued in the mid-1990s.

✎ Examples of "making others feel great" can be found on 3 February, 15 May, and 10 July "touching hearts".

♪ If I am lacking love; Lord have mercy (Give me the heart of stone); Whatsoever you do

10 JUNE

(See also 9 June.)

1 Charles Dickens' book, **'A Tale of Two Cities'** is a novel set in the time of the French Revolution (1789-1799), and the hero of the book travels between the "two cities" of the book's title - London and Paris - to rescue some people who were condemned to die on the guillotine in France.

2 As he set about rescuing those condemned to die, the hero - Sydney Carton - saw both good and bad, and light and darkness in people and situations.

3 Dickens starts '**A Tale of Two Cities**' with these words:
"It was the best of times; it was the worst of times. It was the age of wisdom; it was the age of foolishness... It was the season of light; it was the season of darkness. It was the spring of hope; it was the winter of despair."

4 *Let us pray:*

**Lord, lead me to look for the positive
  in all people
  and in all situations.
May I help bring light
  to those in darkness,
  and encouragement
  to those who feel unhappy.
May I show as much care for others
  as I would like them to show for me.
Amen.**

 Amazing grace; Christ is our king; Lord, make me a means; Make me a channel; Oh the love of my Lord

1 These are some of the impressive achievements of Steven Spielberg as a film director:

Jaws (1975),
Close Encounters of the Third Kind (1977),
Raiders of the Lost Ark (1981),
Indiana Jones and the Temple of Doom (1984),
Who Framed Roger Rabbit (1988),
Indiana Jones and the Last Crusade (1989),
Hook (1991),
Jurassic Park (1993),
Schindler's List (1993),
The Lost World: Jurassic Park (1997),
Amistad (1998).

2 Which famous film is missing from that list?

3 **"E.T. - the Extra-Terrestrial"** was released on this day, 11th June, in 1982. E.T. is left behind on earth - alone and without a friend. His rescuer is a child, and he is sheltered and then rescued by other children. The film is seen from a child's point of view, and all the heroes are children. The film leaves people "feeling good".

4 The direction of these films has been a great achievement - all the more so since Steven Spielberg's schooldays were not happy. He was called names, was 'put down' and laughed at, and was the last to be chosen when everyone had to play in sports teams.

5 *Let us pray:*

Lord Jesus,
   we can read in the Gospel
   of your attitude
   towards those
   whom others looked down on.

6 Zacchaeus, the tax-collector,
   was rejected by others,
   but you called him by his name
   and ate in his house.

7 You did not condemn the woman
   who was about to be stoned
   for adultery,
   but you called her
   to change her life.

8 The woman
   who was drawing water from the well
   was there in the midday heat,
   cut off by others
   because she was a Samaritan.
   Yet she was one of the very few
   whom you told directly
   that you were the Messiah.

9 You have told us
   not to be afraid or anxious,
   and you said that the last will be first.
   You assure us
   that, as God the Father
   even takes care of sparrows,
   we are worth more
   than hundreds of sparrows.

10 We think of people
   being 'put down' or 'bullied'
   and we ask you this day, Lord,
   to remind us of the respect
   that each person deserves.
   Lead us
   to be as encouraging and positive
   to others
   as we would like them to be to us.
   Amen.

✤✿✤✿✤✿✤✿✤✿✤✿✤✿✤✿✤✿✤

🔊 *The prayer is based on:*
   6 - Lk 19$^{1-10}$
   7 - Jn 8$^{1-11}$
   8 - Jn 4$^{5-42}$
   9 - Jn 14^{1}, Mt 20^{16}, Mt 10$^{28-31}$.

 Be not afraid; Here I am, Lord

1 Football was banned in England on this day in 1349. To understand why, we need to know first of all, that the terrible plague of the Black Death had reached England in the previous summer. Fleas living on infected rats carried the disease to humans and animals, killing at least half the population.

2 The terrible disease affected everyone in many ways. Those who did not become ill, suffered the death of loved ones. With only half the people to do the same number of jobs, wages were higher and food prices were lower - but all at such a terrible cost of so many deaths, leaving behind devastated families.

3 With fewer people, would the country - still at war with France - be able to defend itself? King Edward III was very concerned about the defence of the country - particularly the contribution that archers would make. Only three years before, English archers had won the Battle of Crécy against the French. The king knew that people had begun to see life very differently after so many had died of the Black Death. Practising archery was a low priority for them, and they wanted to spend their time doing other things. The king was concerned that the people would lose their skills as archers, and so, on this day in 1349 (a year after the Black Death hit England), King Edward III made a law, banning such sports as football. He proclaimed that every able-bodied man was to spend his spare time practising with a bow and arrow - playing no sport but archery. The archers did regain their skills, and went on to help win the Hundred Years War against France.

4 *Let us pray:*

Help me, Lord,
to discover the talents
I have been given,
and not to let them lie unused
but to make the best use of them
both for myself and for others.
May sport help
to bring out the best in people,
teaching us the lessons
of commitment and co-operation,
of fairness and appreciation.
May sports and hobbies and interests
help me to develop my personality
that I may be renewed and re-created
in your image and likeness. Amen.

✍ *"The Hundred Years War", between England and France, was not fought continuously, but intermittently between 1337 and 1453.*

✍ *The words "re-create" and "recreation" are from the same stem.*

✍ *In 1981, Bill Shankly said: "Some people think football is a matter of life and death. I can assure them it is much more serious than that!"*

✍ *See also 17 May.*

1 Mother Teresa of Calcutta in India heard of a Hindu family having no food, and so she took some rice to them. She tells of looking at the children and seeing hunger in their eyes.

2 The mother of the children was grateful for the rice, and immediately divided it into two and went outside. When the lady returned, Mother Teresa asked her where she had been. *"My neighbours, a Muslim family - they are hungry, too,"* she said. And Mother Teresa told someone later: *" I didn't take any more rice that evening - I wanted them to enjoy the joy of sharing."*

3 *Let us pray:*

Lord Jesus, you said that
"there is more joy in giving
than in receiving".
Inspire us to live generously,
sincerely thinking of others
before ourselves.
May others treat us
as we treat them. Amen.

✍ *"There is more joy in giving than in receiving"*
- a quote of Jesus found in Acts 20[35].

♪ If I am lacking love; I give my hands;
Whatsoever you do

14 JUNE

1 The Guinness Book of Records mentions that in 1869 the Territory of Wyoming in the U.S.A. was the first law-making body to give the vote to women. That was followed by the Isle of Man in 1881. The first country to give votes to women was New Zealand in 1893.

2 Emmeline Pankhurst led the movement in Britain to give the vote to women. It was called the Suffragette Movement. Public meetings and public marches did not seem to advance their cause, and some members took to action that landed them in prison. Emmeline Pankhurst and her daughters Christabel and Sylvia were among those who broke windows so as to be arrested for criminal damage. They saw this as a way of keeping in the public eye the cause of votes for women.

3 Other Suffragettes chained themselves to railings and interrupted political meetings. The home of a senior politician, Lloyd George, was bombed. One woman, Emily Dickinson, was killed as she threw herself under the king's horse at the Derby horse race in 1913.

4 When the First World War started, the Suffragette Movement called off their action. As men went off to war, women took on most of the jobs that the men had been doing. It has been argued that women's actions during the war advanced their cause far more than did the violence. As the War ended in 1918, women over 30 were given the right to vote.

5 On this day in 1928 Emmeline Pankhurst died, a few weeks after full voting rights were given to women.

Let us pray for all who are not given equal opportunities.

Lord, in your mercy - **hear our prayer**.

Let us pray for those who are treated unfairly today, who do not experience justice.

Lord, in your mercy - **hear our prayer**.

Let us pray for a growing awareness of the dignity of each person we will meet today, that we may have as much respect for others as we would like them to have for us.

Lord, in your mercy - **hear our prayer**.

Let us pray for a change of heart in those who abuse others or take advantage of them; those who take people for granted; those who look down on other people; and those who are selfish.

Lord, in your mercy - **hear our prayer.**

📖 Emmeline Pankhurst: 1858 - 14/6/1928

📖 'Suffragettes' - see also 2 June

📖 For 'voting', see also 12 May & Prayer 69 of the Appendix in this volume.

🎵 If I am lacking love; Oh Lord, all the world belongs to you; This is what Yahweh asks of you

1 King John had succeeded to the English throne on the death of his brother, King Richard the Lionheart. John was not a good king, and he abused his powerful position.

2 A group of barons produced a charter (a document), listing what their rights should be, laying down that the king was not to abuse his power and authority in future.

3 The "Magna Carta", as it was called, was signed on this day in 1215. Although King John was reluctant to sign it, the Magna Carta was confirmed by later kings and parliaments. One of its main points is that rulers themselves must live within the law - they are not above it.

4 One of the phrases in the Magna Carta, the 'Great Charter', reads:
   "To no-one
   will we sell or deny or delay
   right or justice."
People were only to be condemned on clear evidence and through a proper trial - things we now take for granted.

5 The Magna Carta also stated that taxes were not to be raised without the consent of those who represent the people, and the Church was to be free from government control.

6 *Let us think and pray:*

Let us pray for individuals who suffer under those who abuse power and people. Let us pray for the defenceless who are treated unfairly and who do not receive justice.

Lord, in your mercy - **hear our prayer.**

7 Let us pray for all rulers, that they appreciate that they are called to serve for the benefit of others.

Lord, in your mercy - **hear our prayer.**

8 Let us pray for our own members of parliament and the government elected by the nation. We pray that they may be people of integrity who govern justly and responsibly.

Lord, in your mercy - **hear our prayer.**

9 Let us pray for ourselves, that we may clearly distinguish good from evil, growing in integrity of character, developing a true sense of values.

Lord, in your mercy - **hear our prayer.**

📖 *In the times of Charles I and Oliver Cromwell and also James II, the principles of the Magna Carta were held firmly by the Parliamentarians, opposing rule by those kings who governed unjustly and irrespective of the law.*

📖 *The Magna Carta was signed in a meadow called Runnymede, near Windsor, outside London. At Runnymede there is another memorial - to the assassinated American President, John F Kennedy.*

📖 *The 'Sermon on the Mount [Mt 5-7; Lk 6[17-49]] - of which the 'Beatitudes' is part - has been called "Jesus' Magna Carta".*

📖 *See 25 June for the U.N. Charter.*

🎵 Come let us go up to the Lord; This is what Yahweh asks of you

1 Florence Nightingale was born in 1820. She felt called to be a nurse and travelled to learn about nursing to many hospitals throughout Britain and Europe.

2 In 1854 the Crimean War started. Britain and France and the Ottoman Empire (based on present-day Turkey) sent armies to resist expansion by the Russian Empire into areas like Romania and Serbia and the Black Sea.

3 Word reached Britain that conditions for the soldiers were dreadful, with supplies of food and clothing never reaching the soldiers. More died of disease than in battle. 'The Times' newspaper wrote: *"Are there no devoted women among us, able and willing to go forth and minister to the sick and suffering soldiers?"* Florence Nightingale volunteered her services, and set off for the Crimea with 38 nurses. On arrival, they discovered that the wounded soldiers were kept in rat-infested buildings. Much of the money that Florence Nightingale was given, she spent on materials to clean the hospital. It was obvious to her that the wounded and sick soldiers had little chance of remaining alive in infected buildings.

4 After 6 months there, Florence Nightingale's efforts greatly reduced the death rate. Before her arrival, 42 out of every 100 patients died; now only 2 out of every 100 died. So grateful were the soldiers for the help and care that Florence Nightingale offered, that many would kiss her shadow as she walked with her lamp through the hospital at night. She became known as *"The Lady with the Lamp"*.

5 She was now a national heroine, and the British public raised £50,000 - a vast amount of money in those times. With that money she founded the first-ever training school for nurses. Yesterday, 15th June, is the anniversary in 1860 of her opening that *'Nightingale School and Home for Nurses'.* From that time on, nurses were well-trained in medical care and the responsibilities of nursing. Florence Nightingale's writings about nursing were translated into many languages. She became the first woman to receive the newly-formed *"Order of Merit"* - an award given by the King or Queen, and limited to 24 people at any one time.

6 Let us pause for a moment to remember in prayer all who are ill, and all who take care of them, mentioning in silence those people whom we know.

(pause...)

✍ *Or could use the prayer of 11 Feb or 28 May.*

✍ *The Crimean War, 1853-1856, centred on resistance mainly by Britain and France to Russia's growing influence in the Balkans [such as Romania and Serbia]. Russia's influence was increasing as the Ottoman Empire [based on Turkey] was collapsing. Russia also wanted to control the straits between the Black Sea and the Mediterranean, giving them influence in the Middle East. The War was named after the Crimean Peninsular - then part of the Russian Empire - where the fighting [e.g. Balaclava] took place. The Crimean War was the first conflict to cost over a million lives.*

✍ *Florence Nightingale: 12/5/1820-13/8/1910. Her first hospital was the converted barracks of Scutari. On her return from the Crimea, she suffered severely from illness herself - thought to be M.E., variously called "Chronic Fatigue Immune Dysfunction Syndrome", which is an incapacitating illness that affects nerve cells, muscle cells, and some of the functions of the brain.*

Poem: "The Charge of the Light Brigade" by Alfred Lord Tennyson.

🎵 Lay your hands; Take my hands; There is a world

1 The body of an adult human contains an incredible 100,000 km (60,000 miles) of blood vessels, and 13 billion nerve cells.

2 An adult has 206 bones. Nearly half of them are found in the hands and feet.

3 The adult human body has about 650 muscles. The smallest muscle is in the ear - only 1 millimetre long. It takes 60 muscles to frown, and only 13 muscles to smile - all the more reason to smile! We're going to listen to some words about the effect of smiling:

4 *"A smile costs nothing*
but gives much.
It enriches those who receive it
without making poorer those who give it.
It takes but a moment,
but the memory of it
sometimes lasts forever.
None is so rich or mighty
that they can get along without it,
and no-one is so poor
that they cannot be made rich by it.

5 *A smile creates happiness in the home,*
fosters goodwill in business,
and is the countersign of friendship.
It brings rest to the weary,
cheerfulness to the discouraged,
sunshine to the sad,
and it is nature's best antidote
in times of trouble.

6 *Yet it cannot be bought, begged,*
borrowed or stolen,
for it is something
that is of no value to anyone
unless it is given away.
Some people are too tired
to give you a smile.
Give them one of yours,
as no-one needs a smile so much
as those who have no more to give."

7 *Let us pray:*

Lord, we give thanks
for all who have brought
life and happiness to us.
Inspire us to give of ourselves joyfully
and always look for the positive.
Amen.

📖 *See also 21 May.*

📖 *A billion is now generally accepted as being one thousand million: 1,000,000,000.*

📖 *At birth, a baby has 300 bones, but 94 fuse/ knit with others. A baby's skull is not fully fused together so as to make it easier for the baby to be delivered.*

📖 *If people rarely see me smile, and if I never smile at a job interview, what conclusions might people draw?*

📖 *The source of the text "A smile costs nothing" is unknown.*

🎼 Give me joy in my heart; I give my hands

1 The majority of mainland Europe was under Napoleon's control by 1812. In that year, he attacked Russia, leading to his downfall and abdication. He was exiled to the island of Elba in the Mediterranean. In March 1815, Napoleon escaped from Elba and returned to France. Men gathered under the French flag, and Europe was threatened with war once more.

2 The British Army, under the Duke of Wellington, approached the village of Waterloo in what is now Belgium. Along with Britain's allies, Wellington was about to engage Napoleon in battle at Waterloo on this day in 1815. A great deal depended on the outcome of the battle as to whether Napoleon would, once again, control all Europe. It could not be forgotten that Napoleon had previously intended to invade Britain. The sooner the news of the battle would reach London, the better. It was decided to send the message by semaphore, from hilltop to hilltop.

3 With semaphore, a person holds a flag in each hand. The position in which each flag is held represents a single letter. Obviously a message can only be read if the person's flags can be seen.

4 For several days a man looked towards the south coast from one of the semaphore points, the tower of Winchester Cathedral. At last, in semaphore, the words of a message were spelt out:

WELLINGTON DEFEATED.

5 At that point a mist swept across, and the watcher could see no more. The disastrous message was then passed on, tower to tower, hilltop to hilltop, all the way to London. It was thought to be a national tragedy.

6 The man on the tower of Winchester Cathedral still kept watch, waiting for the thick mist to clear, hoping to be able to pass on some details of the defeat. After a long time the mist cleared, and the semaphore started again. The first message had read:

WELLINGTON DEFEATED

but as the mist cleared, there were two additional words. Now the full message read:

WELLINGTON DEFEATED THE FRENCH.

7 Those two extra words completely changed the message. What was thought to be defeat was now seen to be victory! The revised message was sent on to London. Church bells pealed, and people cheered in the streets. That deadly first message was only the first part of a message that became good news.

8 We can remind ourselves that, at first, the capture and torture and death of Jesus was disastrous news. All the hopes of his followers had been lost. Three days later the news was completed - it was GOOD NEWS that Jesus had defeated even the power of death, and had risen to new life.

9 *Let us pray:*

Lord Jesus, you overpowered
    the control that sickness had
    by curing people of their illnesses.
Those who were disabled
    were freed to walk again.
You calmed the sea
    and showed that you had control
    over even nature.
You rose to a new way of living
    and showed that not even death
    had power over you.
With your power in our lives,
    everything that happens to us
    can be turned to good.
We ask you this day
    to help us to transform our difficulties
    and draw goodness
    out of what is negative in our lives,
    knowing that there is nothing
    in life or in death
    that can ever separate us
    from your love.
    Amen.

✍ *Napoleon Bonaparte: 1769-1821; Arthur Wellesley, the First Duke of Wellington, was born in the same year, and died in 1852.*

✍ *After Waterloo, Napoleon was finally exiled to the island of St Helena in the South Atlantic, where he died six years later.*

𝄞 For to those who love God; O Lord all the world belongs to you

19 JUNE

(See also 24 June.)

1 Blaise Pascal was born in France on this day in 1623. He is one of the world's greatest mathematicians and scientists. His scientific contributions included work on pressure, and he invented the syringe and the hydraulic press. In tribute to him, the unit of pressure is now called "The Pascal".

2 He made the world's first calculating machine in 1642. He realised that such a machine would help people like his father, who was a tax official. Numbers were dialled on connecting metal wheels, and the result appeared in little windows.

3 Blaise Pascal had an experience that changed the course of his life. Because the experience was so important to him, he wrote about it on a piece of paper, and he sewed that piece of paper into his clothing. There it was found, within his clothing, when he died, nine years later. This is what the paper reads:

4 *"The Year of the Lord, 1654.*
Monday 23rd November,
from about half-past ten in the evening
until about twelve at night: fire.

God of Abraham,
God of Isaac,
God of Jacob
- not the God
of philosophers and scholars.

Certainty, joy, peace.
God of Jesus Christ.
He is only found along the ways
that are taught in the gospel.

Tears of joy.
I had parted from him.
Let me never be separated from him.
Surrender to Jesus Christ."

5 *Let us pray:*

Lord Jesus, you promised
that when two or three
would get together in your name
then you would be present with them.
May your Spirit
lead us to grow more aware
of your presence in our lives
today and every day. Amen.

📖 *Blaise Pascal: 19/6/1623 - 19/8/1662.*

📖 *Pascal's mathematical contributions also included work on 'probabilities', and he left what is called "Pascal's Probabilities Triangle".*

📖 *The Unit of Pressure, 'The Pascal' is one newton per square metre.*

📖 *Pascal's experience was a kind of "transfiguration" - see Matthew 17[1-8].*

🎼 Be still and know I am with you; In you, my God; Oh the love of my Lord

1 England's first Christian martyr was Saint Alban. He was executed in Roman times (about the year 304 A.D.), and the city of St Albans is named after him. The cathedral there is built on the site where he was beheaded. Today is his feastday. Who was Alban, and why did he die?

2 An old man knocked on Alban's door, and he was invited in. The man was a Christian priest who was trying to get away from those who wanted to kill him. Although they had never met before, and even though Alban was not a Christian at that time, he gave food and shelter and protection to the priest, keeping him there in secret. The priest talked about following Christ, and Alban became a Christian although he knew that Christians were being imprisoned or executed.

3 Some time later, the local authorities were told that a priest was hiding in Alban's house, and soldiers were sent to arrest the priest. As the soldiers arrived, Alban wrapped the priest's cloak around himself, wanting the priest to escape. The soldiers took Alban away, thinking he was the priest. Alban was sacrificing himself for the sake of his friend.

4 The Roman governor was angry that he had been cheated of the death of the priest, but he commanded Alban to sacrifice to the Roman gods. Alban refused to do so. After torture, he was executed by being beheaded - simply because he was a Christian.

5 It's unlikely that any of us here will be killed because we are Christians. In other places, people are discriminated against or beaten up or even killed because of their choice to follow Jesus.

6 There is a poster that says: *"If you were accused of being a Christian, would there be enough evidence to convict you?"*

Let's pause in silence for a moment.

(pause...)

7 Let us pray for all prisoners of conscience, and also for those who torture and kill.

Lord, in your mercy - **hear our prayer.**

8 Let us pray that, when times are difficult, others may find us to be true friends.

Lord, in your mercy - **hear our prayer.**

9 Let us pray that we may live generously, being prepared to make sacrifices for the benefit of others.

Lord, in your mercy - **hear our prayer.**

Jn 15^{13}: *"No greater love can someone have than to give up their own life for their friends."*

Abide with me; Christ be beside me; I would be true; Take my hands

21 JUNE

1 21st of June is the longest day of the year. It is called the Summer Solstice.

2 For those living in the northern hemisphere, the Summer Solstice is the day on which the earth, spinning on its axis, has its North Pole 'tipped' as far as it will go to face the sun. Because of this 'tipping' towards the sun, the northern hemisphere receives the longest hours of daylight of the year.

3 *Let us pray:*

Lord God, Creator of light,
at the rising of your sun
each morning,
let the greatest of all lights
- your love -
rise, like the sun,
within my heart.

(from the Armenian Liturgy)

✐ *"Hemisphere" - half of a globe, in this case of the planet*

✐ *The word "solstice" means "sun stands still".*

♦ Colours of day; I watch the sunrise; Morning has broken; Walk with me; Yahweh, I know you are near

JUNE 22

1 Today is the feast of Saints John Fisher and Thomas More. John Fisher was born in Yorkshire, in 1469, and became Bishop of Rochester in Kent. He was well-known as a man of learning, and had written several books. Bishop John Fisher was asked to study the "problem" of the marriage of King Henry VIII *(the eighth)* to Catherine of Aragon. The king wanted to divorce her after 18 years of marriage, in order to have a male successor to the throne. Henry VIII wanted John Fisher and Thomas More (and others) to tell him that he was free to marry again. Both John Fisher and Thomas More were executed for opposing King Henry VIII, who declared himself to be Head of the Church in England.

2 Sometimes when we pray for something, we might think it's an easy way for something to happen, presuming that God will do something without us having to work at it. If I pray for "peace in our world" then I am really also committing myself to start *making* peace around me. Saint Thomas More put this in a simple way when he said:
"The things, good Lord, that we pray for, give us your grace to work for."
We'll make those words our prayer today, as we say:

3 **"The things, good Lord, that we pray for, give us your grace to work for."**

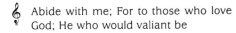

See also 7 February.

Abide with me; For to those who love God; He who would valiant be

77

1 2,000 years ago, some wealthy people would have a statue (or just a head) carved of themselves from marble or stone. It would take a long time and a lot of effort to finish a statue by chipping away with a chisel at the marble or stone. It took only one slip of the chisel for damage to be done. Rather than throw away a damaged statue that had taken so long to produce, some sculptors would melt wax and then mould a little of it into the place where the damage had been.

2 In the sculptor's shop, the customer would not be able to see the wax without looking very closely. In the warmth of a house or the sunshine, the wax might melt. A genuine statue would be **without wax**. The Latin words for *"without wax"* are *"sine cera"* - giving us the English word "sincere". A statue that was "the real thing", genuine, would be *"without wax"* - sincere.

3 And so, if we say that individuals are **not** "sincere", then they are false, not the real thing, not genuine: pretending to be what they are not.

4 *Let us pray:*

Lord, we are conscious
 of the image that people give
 - whether it's the clothes we wear,
 how we look,
 what we say,
 or who we choose to go with.
Sometimes the image doesn't match
 who we really are.
Lead each of us to live sincerely
 as we are called to be. Amen.

"Sine cera" is pronounced "see-nay see-rah"

Romans 12$^{9-18}$: "Do not let your life be a pretence... Let others see that you are interested only in the highest ideals."

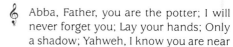

Abba, Father, you are the potter; I will never forget you; Lay your hands; Only a shadow; Yahweh, I know you are near

JUNE 24

(See also 19 June.)

1 Blaise Pascal, one of the world's greatest mathematicians and scientists, once talked of the need for us to pause and rest and think in quietness.

2 He wrote:

"All the troubles of life come upon us
because we refuse to sit quietly
for a while each day,
each of us in our own room."

3 Let's pause in silence for a moment, each with our own thoughts.

(pause...)

4 We'll finish with a prayer written by Blaise Pascal, in which he asks for God's power to do both the little things and the great things of life:

5 *Let us pray:*

Teach us, Lord,
to do the little things
as though they were great,
because of the majesty of Christ
who does them in us
and who lives our life.
Teach us to do the greatest things
as though they were little and easy
because of his great power. Amen.

📖 *Blaise Pascal: 19/6/1623 - 19/8/1662*

📖 *"When you pray, don't be like the hypocrites who make a show of 'praying'. Instead, go into your room where no-one will see you, and close the door, and pray to your Father who sees what is done in secret." - Mt 6$^{5\text{-}6}$.*

📖 *St Augustine of Hippo wrote: "Be great in little things."*

📖 *See 12 July for an appropriate quote of Nelson Mandela.*

📖 *24 June is also the Feast of the Birth of St John the Baptist.*

🎵 Be still and know I am with you; Be still and know that I am God; In you, my God; Oh the love of my Lord

1 Most countries are members of the United Nations.

2 Tomorrow, 26th June, is the anniversary of the signing of the United Nations Charter in 1945, just before the end of the Second World War. The UN Charter is an important statement of what the United Nations commit themselves to do. The Charter includes the following words:

3 *"to maintain international peace and security"*,

4 *"to develop friendly relations among nations"*,

5 *"to achieve international co-operation in solving economic, social, cultural or humanitarian problems"*,

6 *"encouraging respect for human rights and for fundamental problems"*.

7 If justice and peace between nations start with individual people, let's pray for ourselves, that we may commit ourselves each day to live in the same way that we hope that nations will live.

8 Let us pray and commit ourselves that here and amongst our families, we may set out to be understanding, treating everyone fairly.

Lord, in your mercy - *hear our prayer.*

9 Let us pray and commit ourselves to value and respect people as individuals.

Lord, in your mercy - *hear our prayer.*

10 Let us pray and commit ourselves to be positive and friendly and generous towards others.

Lord, in your mercy - *hear our prayer.*

11 Let us pray and commit ourselves not to become prejudiced against people of other backgrounds, religions, or cultures - but may treat others in the same way that we would like them to treat us.

Lord, in your mercy - *hear our prayer.*

📖 *See 15 June for England's "Magna Carta" - Great Charter.*

📖 *The United Nations Charter is not to be confused with the Universal Declaration of Human Rights, of December 1948.*

♪ Come let us go up to the Lord; Let there be peace shared among us; Lord, make me a means; Make me a channel

1 King George IV *(the fourth)* was a heavy drinker. He wasted money and was in debt. He didn't appreciate people, and was unfaithful to his wife. He made fun of his father (King George the III) who had become mentally ill.

2 When King George IV died on this day in 1830, 'The Times' newspaper wrote this about him:
*"There never was an individual
less regretted by his fellow-creatures
than this deceased king."*

3 Many people, when they realise that others have a poor opinion of them, change something in their lives. Let's each of us think in silence for a moment of just **one** thing in our own lives that we might work on improving today.

(pause...)

4 *Let us pray:*

God our Father,
    each of us can rejoice
    at all that is good about ourselves.
We ask that we may be people
    who encourage others,
    being ready to give praise and thanks
    when they are due.
We ask, too,
    that you help each of us today
    to work on changing for the better
    just one thing
    that is negative in the way we live.
Amen.

❖❖❖❖❖❖❖❖❖❖❖❖❖❖❖❖

✍ *What few words might I like to be remembered by? What words about myself might I like to overhear? If I made a coat of arms that would say something about me, what few words or motto might I have as part of my badge e.g. "A faithful friend"; "trustworthy"; "sincere".*

 Lay your hands; Oh the love of my Lord

27 JUNE

1 A World Cup football match was held on this day in 1969 between two countries of Central America. A late penalty was awarded by the referee to El Salvador, against the neighbouring country of Honduras. El Salvador scored from the late penalty, and won the match 3-2. People had become so involved in supporting their national teams that wild riots started in both countries. Opposition fans in each country were beaten up, and looting took place.

2 Six days later - as a direct result of the football match - war broke out between the two countries. Before the war came to an end, two thousand soldiers were killed, and both El Salvador and Honduras suffered severe food shortages.

3 *Let us pray:*

**Lord, there are many places
in our world
where some people do not respect
the background and traditions
and culture of others.
We know that prejudice
can turn to hatred
and even to murder,
and such things often start
in simple ways.
Lead us to live in such a way
that our first reaction
is to think good of people,
focussing on the positive
before we ever see the negative.
Amen.**

📖 *Having beaten Honduras in that round of the World Cup, El Salvador was eliminated in the next round.*

📖 *Words by Grantland Rice, 1880-1954:*
   "For when the One Great Scorer comes
   To write against your name,
   He marks - not that you won or lost -
   But how you played the game."

🎵 Come let us go up to the Lord; If I am lacking love; Lord make me a means; Make me a channel; O Lord, all the world; This is what Yahweh asks of you

JUNE 28

1 On this day in 1914, the Archduke Ferdinand (the heir to the Austro-Hungarian Empire) was assassinated in Sarajevo in Bosnia. This became the spark that started the First World War in which about 19 million people were killed.

2 This also was the day on which the Treaty of Versailles was signed in 1919, at the end of that war. Although the First World War had ended 7 months earlier with an armistice, this treaty formally ended the war, setting severe penalties on those who had lost - particularly Germany.

3 Some parts of the Treaty of Versailles were unjust to Germany. That injustice fuelled the start of the Second World War in which about 60 million people lost their lives.

4 As peace between nations starts with individuals, let's pray first of all that each one of us here appreciates more and more the individuals who are part of our lives. Let's pray that we treat others fairly and with respect.

5 *Let us pray:*

Lord, may peace with justice come to our world, but let peace and justice start with the way each of us lives this day. Amen.

✍ *"Armistice" = a truce, not a surrender. The Armistice in fact ended the War at the 11th hour of the 11th day of the 11th month - 11.00am on 11th November 1918.*

✍ *The number given for the deaths in World War One include civilians who met their deaths indirectly from the war.*

♪ Abide with me; Come let us go up to the Lord; Make me a channel

29 JUNE

1 Today is the feast of Saints Peter and Paul. Who were they?

2 Simon was introduced to Jesus by his brother, Andrew, who was also a fisherman. Later Jesus changed Simon's name to "**PETER**", from the Greek word, 'Petros', meaning "Rock". Peter and his faith would be a rock on which Jesus would build his church, even though Peter would run away and deny knowing Jesus in his hour of need.

3 Peter served as the leader of the first group of Christians. He travelled to the centre of the Roman Empire, and there became the first bishop of the city of Rome. The bishop of Rome is now called the "pope", a word which means "father", recognising his leadership.

4 **PAUL** used to be called "Saul" and had been a Jewish official who hunted down Christians. He was one of those responsible for their deaths, but then had a vision that changed his life, and he became a Christian. Being given a new name, "*Paul*", was a sign of being called to live a new kind of life.

5 We have heard how both Peter and Paul were unlikely choices to help continue the life and work of Jesus - Peter denied knowing Jesus, and Paul had persecuted Christians. Because they are both unlikely characters, and because neither of them was "perfect", we are reminded that God accepts us as we are, with our limitations.

6 Peter and Paul are linked together because, in their different ways, they did so much to inspire and build up the Church.

7 We'll use as a short reading and prayer, some words of Saint Paul, found in a letter that he wrote to the Christians in Rome:

8 **"For those who love God**
   everything works out for good,
   because God has chosen us
   to bear the image of Jesus, his Son.
With God on our side,
   who can be against us?
Even if we face hard times
   or are threatened
   - God's love is greater still,
   and nothing can ever separate us
   from his love.
Through all difficulties
   we can never be failures or losers
   because of the power of God's love."
   (based on Romans 8$^{28-39}$)

*✍ Simon - Peter - Rock ["Cephas" in Aramaic, the language that Jesus spoke]: Mt 16$^{13-19}$ - "You are Peter and on this rock I will build my Church". Catholics tend to reflect on Jesus looking on Peter **himself** as "the rock", whilst Protestants tend to consider that Jesus was referring to Peter's **faith** as "the rock".*

✍ Acts 12$^{1-11}$ tells of the miraculous deliverance of Peter from prison.

✍ Conversion of Saul/Paul: Acts 9$^{1-31}$, 22$^{6-21}$, 26$^{12-18}$ and Galatians 1^{11}-2^{10}.

✍ Acts 8^{1} mentions that "Saul approved of Stephen's murder."

✍ The word "petrol is derived from "petros", rock, as oils formed from the compression underground of tiny organisms over millions of years.

✍ See also 25,26,27 January.

Follow me; For to those who love God; Here I am, Lord; If God is for us; I will be with you

JUNE 30

1 Charles Blondin was a French tightrope walker. On this day in 1859 he first walked across the great Niagara Falls on a tightrope that was 335 metres long (1,100 feet), and 49 metres (160 feet) above the waterfall. With a balancing pole, Charles Blondin walked across in only five minutes. He then crossed back again, blindfolded.

2 Next he walked across pushing a wheelbarrow. When he got to the other side with the wheelbarrow he was congratulated, and one man said to him: *"That's superb! Wonderful!"* Blondin said to him: *"Do you believe I can walk back again with the wheelbarrow?"* *"Yes,"* said the man in great admiration. *"Do you believe I can walk back across the tightrope with someone in that wheelbarrow?"* Again the man said *"Yes, you can do it!"* Then Blondin asked him: *"Will **you** get into the wheelbarrow?"* - but the man refused!

3 The man believed firmly that Blondin **could** take a person back across the tightrope in the wheelbarrow. Believing it, wasn't enough, because there's a difference between 'belief' ("head knowledge") and 'faith' (trust based on experience). He didn't have the personal faith to trust and place himself completely in Blondin's hands.

4 *Let us pray:*

Lord, may I become more aware
of your presence in my life.
May I discover
  that you do walk with me
  each day of my life,
  accompanying me
  in darkness as well as in light,
  in sadness as well as in joy.
May your Spirit lead me
  to trust and come to know

that you keep your word
and are always faithful and loving.
I place myself and my future
into your hands. Amen.

📖 *"Into your hands, Lord, I place myself":* Psalm 31[5]

📖 *The Niagara Falls are on the border between the United States and Canada.*

📖 *Pope Saint Gregory said that* "faith is being a friend of God." *Taking the letters of the word FAITH, it has been said that* "Faith is a Fantastic Adventure In Trusting Him."

📖 *Midnight on 30 June/1 July 1997 saw the transfer of Hong Kong back to China.*

🎵 Christ be beside me; Father, in my life I see; Father, I place into your hands; Walk with me, O my Lord

85

(See also 11 November)

1 Two years into the First World War, the allied leaders hoped that a battle against the Germans based around the River Somme would be decisive: *"the big push"*.

2 For the previous week the German lines had been heavily bombarded. The Allied soldiers were told that there would be so little opposition that many would simply be able to walk across *"no-man's land"* to occupy the German trenches. On 1st July 1916 the Battle of the Somme was launched in bright sunlight at 7.30 in the morning, as thousands of British and Allied soldiers *"went over the top"* along an 18-mile front.

3 The worst casualties ever in a single day in the history of the British Army took place on the 1st July 1916 - over 57,000 British and Empire soldiers were killed on this day.

4 Severe fighting along the Somme took place from 1st July until 18th November, 1916. In that period of 18 weeks:

- 420,000 British and Empire soldiers were killed;

- 200,000 French soldiers;

- and about 600,000 German soldiers lost their lives.

5 *Let us pray:*

**If countries disagree, Lord,
and if negotiations break down,
"going to war"
has sometimes been seen
as a way of "saving face".
In the same way,
there are times
when matters get out of hand
as individuals disagree strongly,
and feel they need to "save face".**

**In my own small part of the world
may I learn ways, Lord,
of being a peacemaker,
of helping people
to see that there are alternatives
to hostility,
and there are ways
of "saving face"
in a decent and human way,
without there being
a break-up of relationships.
Help me
to be a channel of your peace
this day. Amen.**

❖-❖-❖-❖-❖-❖-❖-❖-❖-❖-❖-❖-❖-❖-❖

✍ *The poem 'Dulce et Decorum Est' by Wilfrid Owen, dramatically tells of life in the trenches of the First World War, and the terrible effects of being gassed by chlorine. Also Rupert Brooke's poem, 'The Soldier'.*

Lord, make me a means of your peace;
Make me a channel

2 JULY

1 After the defeat of France at the start of the Second World War, the British Channel Islands were occupied by the Germans on 2nd July 1940.

2 The islands of Jersey, Guernsey, Alderney and Sark were the only British territory occupied by Hitler's troops. The Nazis thought it was good propaganda to be able to show photographs of British policemen saluting German officers, and photographs of German soldiers beside road signs in English.

3 Hitler was convinced that Britain would try to recapture the Channel Islands before or shortly after landing in France on what we now know as 'D-Day'.

4 Hitler had very strong defences put up along the coastline where he thought the Allies might land - along the coast of the Channel Islands, as well as the coast of northern France. The defences were called *"The Atlantic Wall"*, and a quarter of all those defences were around the Channel Islands. Many Russian slave-workers lost their lives in building those defences for the Germans.

5 *Let us pray:*

God our Father,
 in the Bible you tell me
 to *"choose life and not death".*
Inspire me
 in the choices I will make today
 - that I may choose
  what is positive and life-giving
  and good.
So help me to protect and defend myself
 from influences that are not good.
Keep me on the right path
 to choose values
 that are lasting and beneficial.
Keep my eyes open
 whenever there is injustice,
that I may be willing
to stand with those
who are treated unfairly,
and defend those who need support.
Deliver us, Lord, from all that is evil.
Amen.

📖 *See 6 June for 'D-Day'.*

📖 *Although V.E. Day ('Victory in Europe') was 8th May, Liberation Day for the Channel Islands after 5 years' Occupation came the following day.*

📖 *"Choose life and not death" - Deut 30[19]*

📖 *Could include in the prayer the last phrase from Philippians 4[4-9] about filling our minds with everything that is true, noble, good and pure, honourable, virtuous, and worthy of praise (the text is included in 22 February).*

♪ Do not be afraid; He who would valiant be *("thou dost defend us")*; In you, my God; This day God gives me *("God's host defends me")*

1 William Davies was born in Newport, Gwent, on this day in 1871. He was a poet, and wrote:

"What is this life if, full of care,
We have no time to stand and stare?"

2 Let's pray for a growing sense of wonder and appreciation for all that is around us:

Lord God,
may all of your creation
- from the vastness
of mighty stars and planets
to the lowliness
of the smallest living creature I can see
- remind me
to live in wonder and appreciation
of all that is around me. Amen.

"What is this life if, full of care,
We have no time to stand and stare?"

📖 *W.H. Davies: 1871-1940. He crossed the Atlantic several times on cattle boats, and hitch-hiked throughout the United States. He jumped off a train in Canada, injuring a leg which later had to be amputated. When he returned to England he slept rough, and made his living as a street-singer. His poem, "Leisure", was voted 14th in the country's favourite poems on National Poetry Day in 1995. It's in that short poem that we read these words of his. His 14-line poem, "Leisure", can be found in "The Nation's Favourite Poems", ISBN 0-563-38782-3.*

📖 *For some similar ideas, see also 14 July.*

🎼 I watch the sunrise; O Lord my God, when I in awesome wonder

4 JULY

1   On the 4th July - American Independence Day - an American spacecraft called 'Pathfinder' landed on the planet Mars in 1997. The unmanned spacecraft was designed to bounce on landing. The craft later released a moving vehicle the size of a skateboard. It analysed the soil and atmosphere and then automatically transmitted the results back to Earth, by radio signals.

2   Nearly a century earlier, in 1908, the astronomer Percival Lowell announced that he had discovered canals on Mars. He said they were red and seemed to move. We realise now that there are **no** canals on Mars. The great astronomer actually had a rare eye disease - now known as Lowell's Syndrome - which made him see the red veins in his own eyes.

3   Lowell was so famous and such an expert in astronomy that no-one dared to contradict him. Older school atlases still show detailed maps that Lowell charted of his supposed "canals" on Mars!

4   *Let us pray:*
God our Father,
   I can think of mistakes I have made
   and the attitude
   that I have sometimes had.
May I not become so independent
   that I think I know it all
   and no longer need others,
   but may I always
   have true friends around me
   who are willing
   to point me in the right direction.
May I be ready to apologise
   when things go wrong,
   and be ready to learn
   from my mistakes,
   finding humour in my situation
   and having the ability and good sense
   to laugh at myself.
May I grow in wisdom each day.
Amen.

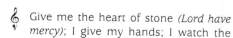 Give me the heart of stone *(Lord have mercy)*; I give my hands; I watch the sunrise; Oh the love of my Lord

1 On this day in 1948 Britain's National Health Service - the N.H.S. - came into being. Before that time, poorer people and their families suffered great financial hardships if a family-member became ill. Since those times, the N.H.S. has grown considerably and offers many services to people.

2 National Insurance is deducted from the wages of those who are working, and that money helps to fund the Service for all who are ill.

3 Many countries see Britain as being blessed with such a fine system of medical care, and most of that care is provided free.

(short pause…)

4 In thinking of those who are sick, we are going to listen to a few sentences of Saint Luke's Gospel. We'll hear about the cure of a sick person - someone who has the skin-disease of leprosy. One of the best ways of reading the gospels is to place ourselves there as one of the characters. We can think of ourselves as the person who is ill and needs help:

5 **Narrator:**

Jesus left the lakeside
and went into one of the villages.
A man appeared, covered with leprosy,
and people kept their distance from him.
He came closer to Jesus
and knelt on the ground before him.
The man with leprosy spoke:

6 **Sick person:**

"Sir, if you want to,
you can cure me."

7 **Narrator:**

What was the reaction of Jesus? He said:

8 **Jesus:**

"Of course I want to
- be cured of what is wrong with you."

9 **Narrator:**

And the man stood up,
and everyone saw that he **was** cured.

10 *Let's pause in silence for a moment*

(pause…)

11 *Let us pray:*

Lord Jesus,
     we hear you say
     that, "of course", you want to heal us
     of what is not good in our lives.
Touch us today
     that we may experience your healing
     and the fullness of your life.
Amen.

📖 *The gospel passage is paraphrased from Luke 5¹²⁻¹⁶.*

📖 *An alternative prayer is that of 11 February.*

📖 *The National Health Service was planned and set up by Aneurin Bevan, under Clement Attlee as Prime Minister, in the government elected in 1945 immediately after the upheavals of the Second World War.*

🎵 Christ is our King; Lay your hands; Walk with me, O my Lord

6 JULY

1 In the 1930s John Dillinger escaped from prison in the United States, having been found guilty of murder and robbery. The F.B.I. identified him as *"Public Enemy Number One"*.

2 Knowing that the police and the F.B.I. had records of his fingerprints, he thought he would set about getting new fingerprints so that his presence would not be detected in future. He dipped his fingers and thumbs into a bowl of acid, and went through great pain until new skin grew. After a few weeks, Dillinger tested his new fingerprints - only to find that they were identical to his old ones.

3 No-one else will ever have the same fingerprints as me. Fingerprints are a sign that each person is unique and individual.

4 *Let us pray:*

God our Father,
you made each of us
unique and unrepeatable.
Inspire me to live in such a way
that I respect others
and am ready to learn
from all who are part of my life
this day.
Amen.

📖 *Oil or perspiration on the ridges that form fingerprints is often transferred as a person touches something. The use of chemicals such as gold particles, and laser treatment, can even highlight faint fingerprints that are a few years old. The 4 main fingerprint types are arch, loop, whorl, and composite. In November 1997, instead of continuing with prisoners giving their fingerprints by using ink, some British police forces adopted laser technology in scanning the fingers of people who have been arrested.*

📖 *"Genetic fingerprinting" is based on the unique DNA "profile" of an individual and, of course, has nothing to do with "fingerprinting" itself.*

📖 *Pope John Paul II has said:*
"Before God,
each human being
is always unique and unrepeatable,
somebody thought of and chosen
from eternity."

📖 *Isaac Newton said:*
"In the absence of any other proof,
the thumb alone would convince me
of God's existence."

🎵 I give my hands; I will never forget you;
Take my hands

1   Muslims have 5 "pillars" in their faith. One of these 5 important duties is to give 2½% of their earnings to charity. It is called *"Zakah"*. This money is specifically to be used to help the poor.

2   We'll use as our prayer today some words based on a Muslim prayer, asking forgiveness for thoughts and words and actions that have been wrong. We also ask forgiveness for **not** having thought and said and done certain things:

3   *Let us pray:*

**For all that we should have thought
    and have not thought;
For all that we should have said
    and have not said;
For all that we should have done,
    and have not done;
we ask forgiveness, Lord.**

4   **For all that we should not have thought
    but have thought;
For all that we should not have said
    but have said;
For all that we should not have done,
    but have done;
we ask forgiveness, Lord.**

All that I am; If I am lacking love; Oh the love of my Lord; Whatsoever you do

8 JULY

1 In 1980 Archbishop Romero was shot dead as he was celebrating Mass in his cathedral in the capital city of the Central American country of El Salvador. He was killed because he complained about the treatment of the poor by the government and army. We can call to mind that the word *"martyr"* is a Greek word meaning *"witness"*.

2 On this day in 1979, just 9 months before he was killed, Archbishop Oscar Romero talked about the witness of Christians, and he even used the phrase *"if they kill your bishop":*

3 *"If some day they take away from us*
our Catholic radio station,
if they close down our newspaper,
if they don't allow us to speak,
if they kill all the priests
and the bishop, too,
and you are left
- a people without priests -
then each one of you
must be God's microphone,
a messenger, a prophet.
The Church will always exist
even if there is only one baptised person.
That one baptised person
would be responsible before the world
for holding up high the banner
of the Lord's truth and justice."

4 *Let us pray:*

Lord our God,
we pray for the strength
to hold to our convictions.
We pray, too,
for the courage and determination
to stand
with those who suffer from injustice.
In all that we do, Lord,
inspire us to act justly,
love tenderly,
and walk humbly with you, our God.
Amen.

📖 For Archbishop Oscar Romero, also see 2 March and 9 July.

📖 The last sentence of the prayer is from the prophet Micah 6^8.

📖 There is a poster that says: "If you were arrested for being a Christian, would there be enough evidence to convict you?"

📖 On this day in 1996 a man armed with a machete attacked a group of children enjoying a teddy-bear's picnic at a primary school in Wolverhampton. 3 children and 4 adults were seriously injured. Miss Lisa Potts protected the children at cost to herself. She was later praised by the judge for her "great unselfishness" and she received the George Medal from the Queen. 13/11/97.

🎵 Abide with me; Colours of day; For those who love God; If God is for us; O Lord all the world; Take my hands; This is what Yahweh

1   Westminster Abbey in London has been used for the coronation of kings and queens. Also held there have been the funerals of members of the Royal Family and great public figures.

2   Some of the spaces above the main entrance of Westminster Abbey have been filled with statues of modern-day saints - unveiled on this day in 1998 in the presence of many church leaders from across the world. It's a very imaginative idea, not least because the statues are of people from different Christian traditions. They include:

3   - Maximilian Kolbe of Poland , a Catholic priest who volunteered to take the place of a married man condemned to death in Auschwitz Concentration Camp in 1941;

4   - Dietrich Bonhoeffer, a Lutheran minister who was part of a plot to kill Hitler, and who was executed by the Nazis in 1945;

5   - Martin Luther King, a Baptist minister and black civil rights campaigner, assassinated in the United States in 1969;

6   - Catholic Archbishop Oscar Romero, gunned down at the altar as he celebrated Mass in his cathedral in El Salvador in 1980;

7   - and Anglican Archbishop Janani Luwum, shot in 1977 in Idi Amin's Uganda.

8   *Let us pray:*

   Loving Lord,
      these individuals we have heard about
   were ordinary people.
   They spent years
      making choices each day
   about small ordinary things.
   Their positive and life-giving attitude
      eventually led to serious decisions
      about standing
      with the poor and the underprivileged
      and those treated unjustly.
   Inspire us, Lord,
      to choose wisely
      in the ordinary circumstances
      of *our* daily lives.
   Having then chosen wisely
      in small things,
      inspire us
      with courage and generosity
      when we must make
      more important decisions. Amen.

❖❖❖❖❖❖❖❖❖❖❖❖❖❖❖❖❖

✐ *An alternative prayer would be that of 7 February.*

✐ *It was in Westminster Abbey that the funeral of Princess Diana was held on 6 September 1997.*

✐ *See 14 August for Maximilian Kolbe; 4 February for Dietrich Bonhoeffer; 15 January, 4/5 April, 29 May, 5 June for Martin Luther King; 24 March and 8 July for Oscar Romero.*

 O Lord all the world; Take my hands; This is what Yahweh asks of you

10 JULY

1. A lady drove to the shopping centre, smiling to herself at the good news she had received about her son. After shopping, she drove out of the car park and handed in her ticket at the kiosk, ready to pay the standard charge of one pound. She opened her purse, smiled, and handed over three £1 coins, saying "This is to pay for the next two cars as well," and then she drove off.

2. What effect might that small gesture have had on the occupants of the next two cars? Somebody they had not met - and would never meet - had acted kindly towards them. They must have thought again about the incident at least once later in the day. Would that lady's action have become like a pebble thrown into water, causing ripples of goodwill and kindness to spread outwards?

3. Someone once said:
"Practice random kindness and senseless acts of beauty."

4. How do some people *"practice random kindness and senseless acts of beauty"* ?
   - being of help to someone they don't know;
   - saying *"Good morning"* to someone they don't normally greet;
   - when feeling negative, going out of their way to do the exact opposite of what they are feeling;
   - doing something that needs to be done, without being asked;
   - noticing when someone doesn't look too happy,and then saying something positive.

5. We are invited to *"practice random kindness and senseless acts of beauty."* Let's reflect and pray in silence for a moment
   (pause...)

> *"Practice random kindness and senseless acts of beauty."*

The quote is from Anne Herbert.

For "random kindness" or "touching hearts" see also 3 February, 15 May, 9 June.

All that I am; If I am lacking love; I give my hands; Oh the love of my Lord; Take my hands

1 When people of the same country fight against each other, that is called a "civil war". Between 1991 and 1995 one of the worst civil wars in history took place. It was in Europe and was between people of the former country of Yugoslavia. Whilst most civil wars are between two groups of people, this was mainly between three groups who fought each other: the Serbs, the Croats and the Bosnian Muslims. Each group reminded the others of events that took place even hundreds of years earlier.

2 The United Nations Organisation declared certain areas to be "safe areas" where no soldiers or civilians were to go into or go out from, and attempts were made to guard these "safe areas" which enclosed Bosnian Muslim groups.

3 This day in 1995 saw the start of atrocities in the so-called "safe area" of the town of Srebrenica. It is estimated that the Serbs massacred about 8,000 people, mainly the men and boys who had been taken away in lorries. Mass graves were later dug up and it was clear that many had not only been murdered but tortured, and their bodies mutilated.

4 Politicians and army leaders had stirred up racial hatred and fears. People thought of the historical events of centuries earlier as though they were taking place in their own time. Evil things were done by each of the three sides during this civil war, which was based on what was called "ethnic cleansing" - towns and whole areas were "cleansed" of people of different racial backgrounds. They were forcibly removed; many families were split up. Rape, torture and murder were widespread.

5 *Let us pray:*

God our Father,
 it seems obvious to many
 that people of all races
 and people of all religions and none
 are brothers and sisters
 of one another.
We ask
 that justice and peace may grow
 in the hearts and minds
 of each individual,
 that we may treat others
 in the same way
 as we wish to be treated.
Rather than thinking over bad things
 that have happened in the past,
 may we grow
 in the freedom, the courage
 and the generosity
 to place past events into your hands.
Teach us
 how to break the cycle of hatred
 by being generous and caring
 towards those
 who have done us harm,
 resisting evil
 and conquering it with good. Amen.

✍ *"Srebrenica" is pronounced "Sreb-re-nit-sa".*

✍ *Until the Fall of Communism, the European Communist country of Yugoslavia was made up of six federal republics: Slovenia, Croatia, Macedonia, Serbia, Bosnia and Herzegovina, and Montenegro. The Serbs tend to be of the Orthodox faith, and the Croats Roman Catholic. The Muslims are either converts or descendants of Turks and others who invaded the area centuries earlier.*

✍ *An alternative prayer would be that of Holy Thursday (printed at the back of volume 1).*

✍ *Romans 12$^{14-21}$ - "Bless those who oppose you. Do not repay evil with evil. Resist evil and conquer it with good."*

🎵 Lord, make me a means of your peace;
Make me a channel of your peace.

12 JULY

1   From the 10th to the 12th July 1996, President Nelson Mandela - the first democratically-elected President of multi-racial South Africa - made a State Visit to Britain. Anyone who makes a State Visit is met by government officials and by the Queen, and banquets are given in that person's honour.

2   In South Africa's days of apartheid - the separation of people according to colour - Nelson Mandela spent many years in prison. After his release and his election, he found himself with very little time for himself. He spoke these words:

3   *"Although it was a tragedy*
    to spend 27 years in prison,
    one of the advantages
    was the ability to sit down and think.
    This is one of the things I miss most."

4   *Let us pray:*

    Lord,
      I want to be responsible
      for my own life,
      and I want to make positive choices
      each day.
    Inspire me
      to get my priorities right
      and be generous
      in my care and concern for others.
    In busy days and casual days
      remind me, too,
      of my basic human need
      for personal time
      and quiet and space,
      and lead me to respect
      the personal needs
      that others also have.
    Amen.

📖 *The prayer above is also used for 27 July. Alternative prayers would be those of 1 April (Slow me down, Lord) and 23 March (the good use of time), and 14 July.*

📖 *In her Christmas Day broadcast that year, the Queen reflected on Nelson Mandela as "that most gracious of men" - see 10 May. See also 27 April and 18 July.*

🎵 Be still and know I am with you; Follow me; God's Spirit is in my heart; In you, my God

1   Yesterday's date, 12th July, was the date on a school report of Winston Churchill, who later became Britain's leader during the Second World War. Churchill was bottom of the class, and a Mr Davidson, his housemaster at Harrow School, wrote on his report:

> *"If you judge people,*
> *you have no time to love them."*

2   *"He is forgetful, careless, unpunctual, irregular in every way...*
If he is unable to conquer this slovenliness he will never make a success..."

3   Some people tend only to judge others and criticise them, never seeing anything positive in them. Mother Teresa said:
"If you judge people,
you have no time to love them."

4   *Let us pray:*

Lord, I ask that you inspire me
    always to do my best
    - not comparing myself with others,
    but only with myself.
Lead me, Lord,
    to discover and use
    my own talents to the full.
May I live in such a way
    that I help others
    to experience success,
    as well as praising them
    for the good use of their abilities
    - looking not so much
    at the degree of achievement
    but at the effort put in.
Stop me from judging people
    or jumping to conclusions
    about them,
    but lead me
    to respect and accept others
    for who they are,
    focussing on the positive
    rather than the negative.
Amen.

✍ *Alternative prayers would be those of 4 March and 2 May.*

♪ Do not be afraid; Father, I place into your hands; O Lord all the world belongs to you; There is a world

14 JULY

1 A fishmerman had landed his catch of fish, cleaned his nets, and was resting by the water's edge, watching the sea, thinking about his day, and enjoying life.

2 A rich man came strolling by. He could see that the fisherman looked relaxed and peaceful, but asked him: "Why are you not working?"

3 The fisherman was surprised at being asked the question, and replied: "I've just finished unloading my catch for the day."

4 "But you've time to go out and get more fish", said the rich man.

5 "Why should I do that?" asked the fisherman.

6 "So that you can sell them and make more money", explained the rich man.

7 "But what would I do with the money?" asked the fisherman.

8 "You could buy a bigger boat," the rich man said.

9 "But why?" asked the fisherman.

10 "Obviously you could catch more fish and make even more money. Then you'd be rich," replied the rich man.

11 "Why would I want to be rich?" asked the poor fisherman.

12 "Then you'd be able to sit back and enjoy life!" remarked the rich man.

13 "But that's exactly what I'm doing now" said the fisherman, sitting by the water's edge.

14 *Let us pray:*

Lord,
I do not want to be selfish.
I *do* realise how important it is
to value and appreciate myself,
and I know
that I need genuine love for myself
if I am fully to love others.
Remind me
of the importance
of keeping time and space and quiet
for myself,
and remind me to respect
the personal needs of others, too.
Lord God,
you who call me by my name,
I thank you for making me
who I am.
Inspire me to grow
as a genuine and sincere person
with a positive attitude,
right values,
and a generous spirit. Amen.

✍ *Pope John Paul II has said:*
"It is not wrong to want to live better; what is wrong is a style of life which is presumed to be better when it is directed towards 'having' rather than 'being'."

✍ *The Greek philosopher, Socrates (about 470-399 B.C.), looking in the market at many goods for sale, said:* "How many things I have no need of."

✍ "The person is nearest to God who needs the fewest things," *said the Roman philosopher Seneca, 4B.C.- 65A.D.*

✍ "... Better deem t'have lived to be, than to have died to have."
(Samuel Daniel, 1563-1619, in 'Musophilus')

✍ *See also 1 April; 3,12,27 July; and the footnotes for 10 August.*

♪ Do not worry; Follow me; God's Spirit is in my heart; O Lord all the world

(See also 16 July.)

1 Wine-producing areas of France lost money whenever their wine went sour. Louis Pasteur discovered that this was due to the presence of micro-organisms, often called bacteria or "germs". He showed that heating sugar solutions before using them would kill off any bacteria.

2 Louis Pasteur also showed that milk can be prevented from going sour if it is first heated to a high temperature under pressure. We now call this "pasteurised milk", after his name.

3 A 9-year old boy, Joseph Meister, was brought to him, having been bitten badly by a rabid dog. Pasteur injected him with a vaccine of a weakened form of the killer disease, produced from the bodies of infected animals. It was on this day in 1885 that young Joseph Meister recovered from the rabies that otherwise would have killed him.

4 Before Pasteur's discoveries about germs, 6 people died out of every 10 who had operations. He started the use of disinfectants to kill germs in operating theatres.

5 The name of Louis Pasteur became widely known throughout France, and he received national honours for his scientific achievements. He was given a state funeral in Paris' Cathedral of Notre Dame.

6 *Let us pray:*

Lord, I need to keep an eye
 on the small things in my life
 as well as the bigger issues,
 because my thoughts
  become my attitude,
 my attitude becomes my words,

my words become my actions,
and my actions form my character.
Be there, Lord,
 in that instant before every thought,
 that I may choose wisely
 my thoughts and my attitude,
 my words and my actions,
 so that I grow
 as the person you call me to be.
Amen.

📖 *Louis Pasteur: 7/12/1822-28/9/1895*

📖 *Perhaps it is understandable that, at first, many people criticised Pasteur for believing that tiny organisms could kill large creatures. It should be realised that many micro-organisms, of course, are beneficial - from bacteria in soil that degrade dead matter, to bacteria cultures in yoghurt.*

📖 *As well as working on the causes and cures for some life-threatening diseases, Pasteur also worked on the polarisation of light by isomers.*

📖 *In 1865 the British doctor, Joseph Lister, came across Pasteur's theories of germs. He used carbolic acid (phenol) to disinfect medical instruments as well as applying it to wounds and surgical dressings. In 1897 Lister was made a Baron by Queen Victoria, who had been one of his patients.*

📖 *See also 14 May*

🎵 Christ be beside me; Do not worry; O Lord all the world

16 JULY

(See also 15 July.)

1 One of France's greatest scientists was Louis Pasteur, who lent his name to the process of "pasteurising" milk. He became well-known in his lifetime, receiving national honours in recognition for his scientific achievements.

2 One day he was travelling by train and was reading the Bible to himself. The man who happened to be sitting next to Louis Pasteur did not know who he was, but saw that he was reading about Jesus feeding 5,000 people with five loaves and two fish. The man said to him: "You don't believe that story, do you?"

3 "Yes, I do believe it," said Pasteur. The other man, not knowing who he was speaking to, said, "Well, *I* don't believe it. I'm a scientist, you see, and that story doesn't fit in with science."

4 At that point the train slowed and the man was about to get off. He said goodbye, giving his name. He was more than surprised to hear in response, "And my name is Louis Pasteur." The man, claiming to be a scientist, had been very dismissive of the religious beliefs of Louis Pasteur, one of the world's greatest scientists.

5 *Let us pray:*

Lord, I ask for the gifts
  of knowledge and wisdom
  and understanding.
What I pray for
  I intend to work at,
  so that I may develop
  an open mind,
  a thirst for knowledge,
  and a wisdom that makes good use
  of my knowledge and experience.

I know that any gifts are useless
  if I do not also have
  love and concern for others,
  and so I ask that you inspire me
  to live in such a way
  that I am caring and compassionate
  and promote understanding
    between people.
May others respect me, Lord,
  as much as I respect them. Amen.

 All that I am; Do not worry; In you, my God; My Lord, my Master; O let all who thirst; O Lord all the world; Seek ye first; Take my hands

JULY 17

1 Two thousand years ago, some leaders of the Roman Empire were called "Caesar". It is from that word that the Germans (at the time of the First World War) named their leader "the Kaiser". Also from the word "Caesar", the Russians called their emperor "the Czar".

2 Nicholas II was the last Russian Czar. He refused to take advice except from his wife, who was under the influence of the mad Rasputin. Nicholas led the country to a disastrous war with Japan in 1904, and he resisted all moves towards any kind of democracy. He gave poor leadership over 23 years, and particularly during the First World War against Germany, when 2 million Russian soldiers died in 1915 alone, and starvation gripped the country. All these factors contributed to the need for a major change. The Russian Revolution took place in 1917 and Communism became the way of life as the country became known as "the Soviet Union".

3 During the night of 16th/17th July 1918, Tsar Nicholas II and his family were killed on the orders of local Soviet officials. After being shot, their bodies were burned and thrown down a mine shaft.

4 After the Fall of Communism in 1991 and the break-up of the Soviet Union, the bones of the Czar and his family were eventually DNA-matched with such distant relatives as Prince Philip, the Duke of Edinburgh. The Russian President, Boris Yeltsin, decreed that the remains of the Russian Royal Family would be buried on 1st March 1998. In the Russian Orthodox Calendar, that day is marked as "Forgiveness Sunday", when people look at their past mistakes, pray for God's forgiveness, and consider how they can make up for what they have done wrong.

5 *Let us pray:*

Loving Lord,
 you tell us in the Bible
 that whatever wrong we have done
 you tread down our faults
 to the bottom of the sea.   Mic 7[19]
We know there is no need
 to keep thinking
 about what we have done
 in the past,   Is 43[18]
 because you pardon
 the wrongs we have done,
 and you delight
 in showing mercy.   Mic 7[18]
You bind up all our wounds   Ps 147[3]
 and you renew us
 by your love.   Zeph 3[17]
Lord, you love
 all that you have made,   Wis 11[24]
 and it is your very nature
 to love and forgive.
Lead us to be generous
 in accepting and forgiving others
 in the same way
 as you accept and forgive us.
Amen.

❖-❖-❖-❖-❖-❖-❖-❖-❖-❖-❖-❖-❖-❖-❖

📖 *"Czar" and "Tsar" are alternative spellings in our alphabet for the same word. A person who is given a lot of power to enforce a law relating to drugs, for example, might be called a "drugs Czar" (or energy czar, etc).*

 Freely, freely; Give me the heart of stone (Lord have mercy); Lay your hands; Oh the love of my Lord; O Lord all the world

18 JULY

1   On this day in 1918 Nelson Mandela was born. On 10th May 1994 he became the first democratically-elected President of multi-racial South Africa.

2   In his inaugural speech as South African President, Nelson Mandela said:

"Our biggest fear
  is not that we are inadequate;
our biggest fear
  is that we are powerful
  beyond measure.
It is our light, not our darkness
  that most frightens us.
We ask ourselves:
'Who am I to be brilliant, gorgeous,
  talented and fabulous'
*Actually, who are you **not** to be?*
You are a child of God.
Your 'playing small'
  doesn't serve the world.
There is nothing enlightened
  about shrinking
  so that other people
  won't feel insecure around you.
We are born to make manifest
  the glory of God that is within us.
It's not just within some of us
  *- it is within **everyone**!*
And as we let our own light shine,
  we consciously give to other people
  permission to do the same.
As we are liberated from our own fear,
  our presence
  automatically liberates others."

3   *Let us pray:*

Lord Jesus,
  bring your love to our lives
  in a new way today
  so that any fear that we might have
  is driven away,
  knowing that
  "perfect love casts out fear".

Then your light
  will shine more brightly in us,
  and others will be able to see
  the good things that are done
  in your name.
Help us to grow more aware
  of the love and respect and dignity
  that you give us
  in calling us your "friends".
We ask that your Spirit acts in us
  so that we discover
  and take pride
  in who we really are.
Make us credible witnesses
  of your love
  so that others
  may more readily share
  in your love and your light,
  you who are the light of the world.
Amen.

📖 *See 23 February for some similar ideas.*

📖 *Regarding Nelson Mandela, see also 27 April, 10 May, 12 July.*

📖 *"Let your light so shine before others that they will give the praise to your Father in heaven"*
          -Mt 5[16]
"Perfect love casts out fear" - 1 John 4[18]
"I call you friends" - Jn 15[14]
"Light of the world" - Jn 8[12]

🎼 Colours of day; Come, come, follow me; Do not worry; Father, I place into your hands; I watch the sunrise; O Lord, all the world

1 At the 1992 Olympics in Barcelona, Spain, one of Britain's athletes - Derek Redmond - was running in the semi-final of the 400 metre race. As he rounded the curve he could see the finishing line. Suddenly a very sharp pain in the back of his leg caused him to collapse on the racetrack. It was a torn right hamstring.

2 Medical people ran towards him, but Derek Redmond struggled to his feet and started hopping on one leg. He was determined to finish the race, even though he was in great pain and the other runners had passed the finishing line. As he got a few metres down the track, a man came out of the stands and ran past a security guard and onto the track. It was Jim Redmond, Derek's father. *"You don't have to do this"*, he told his son. *"Yes I do"*, said the athlete. *"Well then, we'll finish it together,"* said his father.

3 With his arm around his father's neck, Derek hopped around the rest of his lane to the finishing line. By this time the people in the crowd were on their feet, clapping for the courage and the spirit both of Derek Redmond and of his father.

4 *Let us pray:*

In times of difficulty, Lord, may we support others with the same care and concern as we would like to experience ourselves. Amen.

📖 *See also 23 July.*

📖 *Such warm support of a father is reflected in Jesus' story of the Prodigal Son. The father "ran toward his son and clasped him in his arms". That expressively compassionate warm embrace given by the father is an image of God the Father - see Luke 15$^{11-32}$.*

🎵 Do not worry *("go do your best today")*; I give my hands; Though the mountains may fall *("shall run and never tire")*; Walk with me, oh my Lord; Yahweh I know you are near *("where can I run from your love?")*

20 JULY

1 This was a momentous day in 1969 because TV pictures showed two people walking on the moon for the first time.

2 Apollo 11 had blasted off from Earth four days earlier. On this day hundreds of millions of television viewers across the world watched as their lunar module separated from the command module of Apollo 11, which continued to orbit the moon. The scenes, beamed back to Earth, showed the moon's surface becoming larger until the lunar module came to rest on an area of land called the Tranquillity Sea.

3 Neil Armstrong's words to the Command Centre back in Houston, Texas, were heard by millions:
"Houston. This is Tranquility Base. The Eagle has landed!"

4 A little later Neil Armstrong descended the ladder. As he left the last rung of the ladder, he said:
"That's one small step for a man; one giant leap for mankind."

5. They collected 21 kg (47 lbs) of rock samples to return to the Earth, and they planted the American flag on the moon, saying that they landed there in peace and for all mankind. They also left behind on the moon a small sealed capsule which contains the words of one of the prayers of the Bible. It is Psalm 8, and we'll use that as our prayer today:

6 *Let us pray:*

**Lord, our God and King,
your greatness is seen
throughout the earth.**

7 **When I gaze at the heavens
which your fingers have formed,
and look at the moon and the stars
which you have set there,**

I realise how small we are
in the majesty of your creation.

8 **Yet you treasure us
above all that you have made,
and you give us control
over all the works of your hand
- animals both wild and tame,
birds in the air,
and the creatures of the sea.**

9 **Lord, our God and King,
your greatness is seen
throughout the earth.**

✍ *See also 21,22,25 July.*

🎵 I watch the sunrise; O Lord my God, the Father of creation; O Lord my God, when I in awesome wonder; Yahweh I know you are near

1 After landing on the moon on the 20th July 1969, it was a few hours before Neil Armstrong stepped out onto the moon, followed by Edwin "Buzz" Aldrin. Aldrin later wrote about something he did during those few hours:

2 *"There are many thousands of things*
that God and man
have made here on earth
and, before I blasted off,
I got thinking and wondering
what I would choose
to take to the moon.
So I said:
What's our greatest treasure
here on earth?
And I thought:
It's Christ's gift of himself.
So, shortly after touchdown,
I opened two little plastic packages,
one containing bread
and the other, wine.
I poured the wine into the chalice
which our home church had given me,
and I read what Saint John tells us
that Jesus said:
'I am the vine,
you are the branches.'
In the one-sixth gravity of the moon
the wine curled slowly and gracefully
up the side of the cup.
It was interesting to think
that the very first liquid
ever poured on the moon
and the very first food eaten there
were what Christ chose
when he gave himself
to be our close friend."

3 *Let us pray:*

God our Father,
the landing on the moon
was one of the most significant events
in human history.

We give thanks
for the skills and expertise
and the courage and co-operation
which led
to that successful venture.
In giving thanks
we recall, too,
that the astronauts
showed their appreciation
and reminded us
of important values.
We pray for the power of your Spirit
in our lives
that we may live in thankfulness
and be people of vision and courage
who have compassion for one another.
Amen.

❖❖❖❖❖❖❖❖❖❖❖❖❖❖❖❖❖

 *See also 20,22,25 July*

In memory of Jesus; I watch the sunrise; Lord Jesus Christ, you have come to us; My Lord, my Master *(bread and wine as food for the journey)*; O Lord my God, the Father of creation; O Lord my God, when I in awesome wonder; Yahweh I know you are near

1 The science-fiction writer, Arthur C. Clarke, estimated that 300,000 people contributed in different ways so that Neil Armstrong and Buzz Aldrin became the first people to walk on the moon in 1969.

> "God's Word became a human being, and he lived among us."
> Jn 1:14

2 Of those 300,000 people, a group of technicians built the lunar landing craft. To name their vehicle they chose the letters and numbers "JN 1-14". They were asked to explain their unusual choice.

3 The technicians said that, like everyone else, they were very aware of the significance of landing on the moon. As a group of Christians, they wanted to call to mind that there was something even more significant and special in human history. So they named the moon's landing craft after the gospel passage of Saint John, chapter 1, verse 14 - "JN 1-14", which reads:
"God's Word became a human being, and he lived among us."

4 *Let us pray:*

God our Father,
we thank you
that in the vastness of your creation
there is something special
about the beauty of this earth.
Into our world
which you love so much
you sent Jesus, your Son
- your Word
who became a human being -
and he made his home among us.
Open our eyes
that we may have
a sense of wonder and awe
that leads us to treasure
all that you have made.
Show us how to value
all who are a part of our lives this day.
Amen.

📖 *Arthur C Clarke, a former radar instructor in the Royal Air Force, is perhaps best remembered for his book, "2001: A Space Odyssey", later developed into a film by Stanley Kubrick. Clarke is the person who came up with the idea of satellites that would be "geo-stationary" or in "geosynchronous" orbit i.e. although they travel around the Earth, they do so at such a speed as to match that of the land below. There are now hundreds of communications satellites in geosynchronous orbit - they follow a circular orbit over the equator at a height of 35,800 km (22,300 miles). The satellites can be used to receive signals (the 'uplink') from one ground station, amplify the signal, and then re-transmit the signal at a different frequency (the 'downlink') to another station. By this means TV, radio and telephone communications are beamed around the world. If laser signals are used in the blue-green wavelength (which penetrates water) then communication may be held with submarines under the water.*

📖 *The prayer called "the Angelus" reflects in part on the message of the gospel passage of Jn 1[14].*

📖 *Michael Collins (who stayed in lunar orbit) said that*
"the beauty of the planet
from 100,000 miles
should be a goal for all of us,
to help in our struggle
to make it as it appears to be."

📖 *See also 20,21,25 July.*

🎼 I watch the sunrise; Look at the sky;

(See also 6 April.)

1 The 1996 Olympics were held in Atlanta, Georgia, in the United States. One of the most memorable parts of the Opening Ceremony was that of Mohammed Ali lighting the Olympic Flame. Ali had been the greatest boxer in the world, but then developed Parkinson's Disease. At the Opening Ceremony he was seen by millions of people world-wide, uncontrollably shaking because of the disease. His willingness to appear seemed to convey to many people the true spirit and courage of "the Olympic dream". He was later awarded an honorary gold medal.

2 On this day at those Games in Atlanta in 1996, 18 year-old Kerry Strug was determined to help win an Olympic gold medal for her gymnast team. She had a twisted ankle but still wanted to perform her vault, so as not to let the others down. As she landed, she collapsed in pain, but she was remembered for struggling with her difficulty to achieve the gold medal for her team.

3 *Let us pray:*

We pray, Lord,
    for all who will need
    strength and courage today:
- for those who are seriously ill;
- for those
    who are in desperate situations
    and see no hope of anything different;
- for those who find it difficult
    to face others or themselves;
- for those in pain from illness
    or mistreatment or torture;
- for those who know
    that others depend on them.
For all these people
    we ask for the power of your Spirit
    in their lives.
Amen.

Do not worry *("go do your best today")*; I give my hands; Though the mountains may fall *("shall run and never tire")*; Walk with me, oh my Lord; Yahweh I know you are near *("where can I run from your love?")*

24 JULY

1 The words of the song *"Amazing Grace"* were written by John Newton, who was born on this day in 1725. His father was a ship's captain, and his mother died when he was 7. He attended a boarding school and was so badly treated there that he ran away to sea. There he lived a very rough life, and found himself "press-ganged" - forced to join a ship of the Royal Navy. Having escaped and been imprisoned, he got work on a slave-ship.

2 By accident he came across a book called *"The Imitation of Christ"*, and he began to think seriously about his life. A very violent storm almost capsized his ship and, wrongly, he thought that he was "too late" to turn to God. The following morning he was a changed person. He became a preacher, and his most famous hymn is *"Amazing grace"*. He talks of *"many dangers, toils and snares"* that he has already come through. The word *"grace"* is sometimes used to mean God's power in a person's life.

3 We use the words of John Newton's hymn as our prayer today, asking that we may be aware of God's amazing grace in our daily lives:

4 **Amazing grace! How sweet the sound that saved a wretch like me.**
I once was lost, but now I'm found;
was blind, but now I see.

5 'Twas grace that taught my heart to fear, and grace my fears relieved.
How precious did that grace appear the hour I first believed.

6 Through many dangers, toils and snares I have already come.
'Tis grace hath brought me safe thus far, and grace will lead me home.

7 **The Lord has promised good to me;**
his word my hope secures.
He will my shield and portion be as long as life endures.

📖 *"Lost and found"* - Chapter 15 of St Luke's Gospel has three "lost" parables - the lost sheep, the lost coin, and the lost (prodigal) son.

📖 *Roger Garaudy wrote about Jesus:*
"I do not know much about this Man, but I do know
that his life conveys this one message:
'Anyone can, at any moment, start a new future.'"

1 When the three Apollo 11 astronauts returned to Earth after their moon landing in 1969, many nations wanted to welcome them. Neil Armstrong, Edwin "Buzz" Aldrin and Michael Collins made a tour of many countries. Arriving in Italy they also visited the Pope in Rome.

2 Pope Paul VI *(the sixth)* presented them with porcelain statues of the Three Wise Men who had followed the star to find Jesus in Bethlehem. Buzz Aldrin later said that this was one of the most moving moments of their 23-nation tour, as Pope Paul compared them with the Three Wise Men who visited Jesus at his birth, saying that the three astronauts, too, had reached their destination by following the stars that they could see. For the astronauts, it was only by focusing on certain stars that the computer's navigation system and the gyroscopes could lead them to their destiny.

3 Some schools have a star as part of their uniform badge. The star can be a sign of faith, representing the vision of the Wise Men who followed God's sign and discovered the birth of Jesus in Bethlehem.

4 *Let us pray:*

God our Father,
the star of Bethlehem
was a sign of faith
for the Wise Men,
and their faith led them
to discover the newly-born Jesus
in Bethlehem.
May we grow in faith
and discover Jesus
in our daily lives.
Lord, hear us
Lord, graciously hear us.

5 **Thousands of people worked together**
to enable the astronauts
to land on the moon.
May we grow in our appreciation
for all who are part of our lives.
Lord, hear us
Lord, graciously hear us.

6 **The Wise Men**
had a sense of vision and purpose
- and so did the astronauts.
Give us the power of your Holy Spirit
that we may share your vision
of individuals and of our world.
Lord, hear us
Lord, graciously hear us.

✍ *See also 5,6,7 January, and 20,21,22 July.*

✍ *The astronauts presented Pope Paul with a sample of the moon rock they had brought back. It can now be seen on exhibition in the Vatican Museums. Another sample is sealed into one of the stained-glass windows of Washington Cathedral.*

✍ *It should be remembered that the astronauts couldn't navigate to get to the moon by pointing their ship at the moon - the moon, of course, moves in orbit around the earth. They had to navigate according to the position of the stars, directing themselves to where the moon would be at a certain time on a certain date.*

♪ Come and join the celebration; I watch the sunrise; Lord Jesus Christ, you have come to us; O Lord my God, the Father of creation; O Lord my God, when I in awesome wonder

1 George Bernard Shaw is thought of by many as one of the greatest writers of plays in the English language. He was born in Dublin on this day in 1856, and was awarded the Nobel Prize for Literature in 1925. Like Charles Dickens, his writings often expressed the need for changes in society.

2 One of George Bernard Shaw's plays is called 'Pygmalion'. It tells of a Cockney girl, Eliza Doolittle, who sold flowers on the streets of London. As a kind of "experiment" to see how people can change, she is taken to a different place and given fine clothes to wear. She is taught to speak and behave like a lady. One of the characters in the story is a Professor Higgins who treats her as though she is still a flower girl. Eliza speaks these words to Colonel Pickering who treats her like a **lady**:

3 *"The difference*
between a lady and a flower-girl
is not how she behaves,
but how she's treated.
I shall always be a flower-girl
to Professor Higgins,
*because he always **treats** me*
as a flower-girl, and always will.
But I know I can be a lady to you,
*because you always **treat** me as a lady,*
and always will.

4 *Let us pray:*

Lord, may I receive this day
as much respect and encouragement
and building up
as I give to others today.
Amen.

📖 *George Bernard Shaw's play, 'Pygmalion', also became popular as a film and then as the basis for a musical comedy named "My Fair Lady".*

📖 *See also 1 February for a similar theme.*

🎵 Come, come, follow me; Do not be afraid; Do not worry *("go do your best today")*; Follow me; Happy the man; If I am lacking love; Sing a simple song; The love I have for you

1 Yesterday, 26th July, was the anniversary of the birth in 1875 of Carl Jung, who became a world-famous psychologist - someone who studies human behaviour and is able to share thoughts about why people do certain things.

2 People made appointments to see Carl Jung at his home in Switzerland so that they could talk through their problems. One day a wealthy lady phoned him to request an urgent appointment the following day at 3.00 in the afternoon. He said that it wouldn't be possible because he was already committed to an important appointment at that time.

3 The following day, at the time the lady would have liked her appointment with Doctor Jung, she happened to be in a boat sailing past his garden which led down to the shore of the Lake of Zurich. There she could see him, sitting on a low wall with his shoes and socks off, dangling his feet in the water. She was angry - he had lied to her, she said to herself. He'd had no appointment at all!

4 When she arrived home she was still angry and phoned him again: *"You said that you couldn't see me because you had a very important engagement. But I saw you at that very time, doing nothing but sitting on the shore of the lake by yourself."*

5 Jung replied: *"I told you no lie. I had an appointment. It was the most important appointment of the week - an appointment with myself."*

6 *Let us pray:*

Lord,
I want to be responsible
for my own life,
and I want to make positive choices
each day.

Inspire me to get my priorities right
and be generous
in my care and concern for others.
In busy days and casual days
remind me, too,
of my basic human need
for personal time and quiet and space,
and lead me to respect
the personal needs
that others also have.
Amen.

✥✥✥✥✥✥✥✥✥✥✥✥✥✥✥✥✥

📖 *Carl Jung: (26/7/1875 - 6/6/1961)*

📖 *The name "Jung" is identical in pronunciation to the word "young". Carl Jung wrote: "In 30 years I have treated many patients. Among all my patients in the second half of their lives, every one of them fell ill because he had lost that which the living religions of every age had given their followers, and none of them was really healed who did not regain his religious outlook."*

📖 *The prayer is the same as that for 12 July. For similar ideas as to this theme, see 1 April; 3, 12, 14 July.*

📖 *The Anglican bishop, Jeremy Taylor (1613-1667) wrote:*
"There should be in the soul
halls of space,
avenues of leisure,
and high porticos of silence,
where God walks."

📖 *Poem: The Lake Isle of Innisfree by W.B. Yeats.*

🎵 Do not worry; Father, I place into your hands; Happy the man; I will never forget you; Lay your hands; The love I have for you

1 In the 16th Century, European explorers brought to Europe some potatoes from the Andes mountain region in the country we now call Peru, in South America. One of these was Sir Walter Raleigh who was a politician in the reign of Queen Elizabeth I. This is reputed to be the day in 1586 when Sir Walter Raleigh was the first to plant potatoes in Europe.

2 Nearly 300 years later, in 1853, an awkward customer was eating chips in a very smart restaurant in the United States. The customer complained that the chips were too thick, soggy and not salty enough, and had them sent back to the chef, George Crum, who had some thinner chips cooked for the customer. Still he didn't like them, and said that he had recently been in Paris where the chips were thinner. The customer's words *"Tell the chef to try again!"* reached George Crum and infuriated him!

3 In anger, he cut a potato into the thinnest slices he could make, and then soaked them in salted ice-water for 30 minutes, wanting to annoy the customer by making him wait. Then he dropped the very thin potato slices into boiling fat, and they came out crisp and golden. He took them himself to the awkward customer, who tasted them and said they were delicious!

4 In the cook's anger, and quite by accident, what we call "potato crisps" were discovered! The Americans call them "potato chips", as they were first cooked as chips.

5 *Let us pray:*

**There are times, Lord,
  when we say we are hungry
but we really have no idea
what real hunger is,
and the desperation
that goes with it.
We even tend to waste food.
We ask you, Lord, to inspire us
  to discover the real priorities in life
so that we may live simply
so that others may simply live.
Amen.**

❖⬦❖⬦❖⬦❖⬦❖⬦❖⬦❖⬦❖⬦❖⬦❖

📖 *William Raleigh presented some potatoes to Queen Elizabeth I to plant in the garden and grow. Some months later the servants were about to serve the Queen with a salad made from the potato leaves, when Walter Raleigh pointed out that it was the tubers (the potatoes themselves) that were to be eaten. In fact, the leaves are poisonous.*

📖 *There are now more than 150 varieties of potato.*

📖 *Gandhi once said:*
  *"In India
  we have got three million people
  having to be satisfied
  with one meal a day,
  and that meal consists
  of unleavened bread - chapati -
  containing no fat in it,
  and a pinch of salt.
  You and I must adjust our wants
  so that they
  may be nursed, fed and clothed."*

📖 *An alternative prayer would be that of 16 March.*

🎵 O Lord all the world belongs to you; My Lord, my master (*"food for the journey"*)

1 When he was aged 14, William Wilberforce wrote a letter to a newspaper to say how evil it was to trade in slaves.

2 He became Member of Parliament for Hull in 1780, and he was determined to fight against slavery. Many people opposed him - especially those who made a profit from the slave trade, such as those involved in importing sugar from the West Indies. Eventually, in 1807, he convinced the British Parliament to ban the slave trade. Just before he died, a law was passed to free slaves throughout the British Empire.

3 William Wilberforce died on this day in 1833 and was given a public funeral and buried in Westminster Abbey.

4 *Let us pray:*

Lord Jesus,
   the Bible reminds us
   of the dignity and equality
   of all people,
   and you call us to love our neighbours
   as we love ourselves.
At the beginning of your ministry
   you read out loud
   in the synagogue of Nazareth
   from the prophet, Isaiah,
   saying:
   "I have been sent to give liberty
   to the captives."
Today we will meet people
   who are held captive in different ways
   by being treated unfairly,
   or abused, taken for granted,
   overworked, looked down upon.
Be with us, Lord,
   that we may help
   to bring freedom today
   by giving respect and support
   and encouragement.   Amen.

In 1781 a slave ship set sail from the west African coast, on the way to Jamaica. It had been packed with 440 slaves, chained together. On the journey a disease broke out and 60 of the slaves died. Their bodies were thrown into the sea. Others were ill, and the captain decided to throw the remaining slaves overboard whilst still alive, and then claim from the insurance company, alleging that the ship had run out of fresh water. Once in the water, one of the slaves managed to catch hold of a rope and struggled back on to the ship, where he hid.

When the ship reached England the slave told his account of the murders. The insurance company would not pay the money that the slaves were "worth", and the matter went to court. The judge decreed that the slaves were the property of the owners, saying "It is only like throwing horses overboard."

This terrible incident and the underlying prejudice and disregard for human beings helped many to really see just how evil slavery was. A politician who was determined to defeat slavery was the M.P. for Hull, William Wilberforce.

Regarding slavery, see also 9 April and 24 July.

Steven Spielberg's moving film 'Amistad' (1998) concerned slavery.

Denmark had been the first European country to ban the slave trade - in 1792. Britain followed in 1807.

Could also think of and pray for named hostages throughout the world, perhaps lighting a candle for them. Look up in the index the name of 'Terry Waite', the former hostage.

Amazing grace; Christ is our king; God's Spirit is in my heart *(He sent me to give)*; Moses I know you're the man

30 JULY

1 In the 1994 World Cup, Andrés Escobar played for Colombia. He scored an own goal which resulted in his country being eliminated from the World Cup. Because of this, Escobar was murdered on his return to Colombia.

2 On a happier note, this was the day in 1966 when England played West Germany in the final of the World Cup at Wembley. At 3-2 for England the final whistle was about to blow, and people were cheering as though the match had ended. The commentator said *"They think it's all over"* and suddenly England scored again in the last few seconds. *"It is now"*, added the commentator, and England beat West Germany 4-2.

3 Playing for Brazil in that same World Cup in 1966 was Pele, one of the finest footballers ever. He began playing international games at the age of 16. Pele said: *"I regard my skills as a gift from God."*

4 *Let us pray:*

Lord God, I thank you
   for your gifts to me
   of skills, talents, and abilities.
May I use them
   to the best of my ability
   and grow as the person
   you want me to be.
Amen.

 Father, I place into your hands; I give my hands; Take my hands

1 If we look at the outside of some houses that are more than 150 years old, we can often see that at least one window has been bricked up. Why was this?

2 In 1696 the "Window Tax" became law - it was a new way of raising money for the government of the day. This was a tax on each window - the more windows, the more money had to be paid in tax. Wealthy people could afford to pay, and so they didn't have to block any windows. Poor people and the less well-off could not afford the tax. Their only option was to brick up a window or two and have less light in the house.

3 A week ago - 24th July - marked the anniversary of the repeal of (the doing away with) the Window Tax in 1851.

4 *Let us pray:*

God our Father,
   it was Pope John the Twenty-Third
   who was speaking about the need
      to bring new life to the Church.
To illustrate his point,
   he walked to his window
   and opened it wide,
   saying that fresh air was needed
   to blow away the cobwebs
   and refreshen the Church.
Father, do not let us
   shut ourselves off from others,
   but may the windows
   of our hearts and minds be open,
   so that we may be made new
   by your Holy Spirit
   and be influenced for good.
Inspire us, too,
   to let our light shine out,
   knowing that Jesus said
      that we are the light of the world.
Amen.

🖎 *The Window Tax was brought in under King William III (of Orange). Originally it was to bring in extra money to pay for the replacement of damaged coins. 100 years later the then Prime Minister - Pitt the Younger - increased this tax, and even more windows were bricked up! Another 50 years later the hated tax was repealed on 24th July in 1851.*

🖎 *Mt 5$^{14-16}$:* "You are the light of the world... Let your light shine before others so that, seeing your good works, they may praise your Father in heaven."

🖎 *Acts 20$^{7-12}$ - The young man, Eutychus, sitting on a window-sill, drops off to sleep as Paul preaches, falling out of the upstairs window. Paul prays and he comes back to life.*

🖎 *Acts 2$^{1-13}$:* "they heard what sounded like a powerful wind from heaven" - *the coming of the Holy Spirit at Pentecost.*

🖎 *Queen Elizabeth I (1533-1603), regarding respect for the conscience of each individual, said: "I would not open windows into men's souls."*

🖎 *The historical incident known as the "Defenestration of Prague" - when Czechs threw out of the window two diplomats from the Hapsburg rulers - led to the Thirty Years War (1618-1648).*

🖎 *John XXIII was Pope from 1958-1963.*

🖎 *Today is the feast of St Ignatius Loyola - see 31 March.*

♪ Colours of day; I watch the sunrise; The light of Christ

1 When Pope John Paul celebrated Mass in Manchester in 1982, he wore a vestment embroidered on the back with the following square of 25 letters:

R O T A S
O P E R A
T E N E T
A R E P O
S A T O R

2 The word "ROTAS" can be read across the top line, down from the top-left, backwards along the bottom line, and upwards from the bottom right-hand corner. The same can be done with the other words.

3 The words are Latin. The five words can be translated: *"Arepo, the sower, guides the wheels carefully!"* It seems a strange message for the Pope to be wearing on his clothing during his visit to Manchester!

4 It is, in fact, a secret Christian sign. Just 4 years before the Pope's Visit, a vase with these words on it was unearthed in Manchester. The vase dates back to about 180AD, showing that there were Christians living in the area at that early time.

5 What is the Latin for the two words that start the Lord's prayer (i.e. "Our Father")?

6 *"Pater noster"* are the words that start the prayer in Latin, which was the main language for people at the time of the Roman Empire.

7 In the 25-letter word square we could cross off the 11 letters of the two words *"Pater noster"*. We are left with 14 letters.

8 Let's try crossing out the letters of *"Pater noster"* once again. We find that we are short of a letter "N", and we have two A's left over, and two O's. How might we write down *"Pater noster"* twice, using the letter only once?

9 We could write the words *"Pater noster"* across the page and then down the page if we use the single letter "N" for both sets of words. The words now appear in the shape of a cross - itself a Christian symbol.

10 Where are the letters "A" and "O" sometimes seen together?

11 "A" and "O" are two letters sometimes found on candles or vestments or on the front of an altar. In those places they usually appear as Greek capital letters: "alpha" and "omega" - A and Ω. They are the first and last letters of the alphabet in Greek, which was another language spoken in the Roman Empire. Christians knew of references in the New Testament to Jesus as *"the alpha and the omega, the beginning and the end."* Our four spare letters - two A's and two O's, we can place at the ends of each arm of the cross we have made from the words *"Pater noster".*

12 It was in the summer of 1978, during excavation work in Manchester city centre, that part of a two-handled Roman vase was found, bearing the 25-letter square. The vase was dated to 180-190AD. This means that there were Christians living in northern England only 150 years after the death and Resurrection of Jesus!

```
                A
                P
                A
                T
                E
                R
A  P A T E R N O S T E R  O
                O
                S
                T
                E
                R
                O
```

13 *Let us pray:*

God our Father,
   if I could trace back
   through the last two thousand years,
   marking out routes
   from Jesus himself
   and then through people
   whose faith has touched others
   and so reached me,
   I would be astounded
   by the individuals I would encounter.
I give thanks, Father,
   for all those people
   over two thousand years
   who have inspired others
   and played their part
   in passing on
   to generation after generation
   the living heritage of their faith.
Especially I give thanks
   for those who have lived their faith
   through difficulties
   and hardship and persecution.
I pray, Father, that I may grow
   in your faith and love
   through good times and bad.
   Amen.

📖 *Can tease out what the Latin might be for "Our Father" by reference to "paternal" grandparents being the parents of one's father.*

📖 *The words O and A and A and O are found in verse 5 of the Christmas carol, "Unto us is born a Son". "I am the Alpha and the Omega" can be found in Revelation (Apocalypse) 21⁶, and also Rev 1⁴⁻⁸ and 22¹³. The words can be understood to mean that Jesus is present with us at the beginning and throughout and at the end of our day/work/life - he is always with us. The Greek letters A and Ω may be seen on the Paschal candle used at Easter and seen at baptisms and funerals.*

📖 *The 25-letter cryptogram had previously been found (and deciphered) in six places around the world. It was found on a wall in Pompeii that was covered by the volcanic eruption of Vesuvius on 24 August in 79A.D. It was also found on a tile at Budapest on the River Danube; on a scrap of leather in Saxony, Germany; at Dura Europos, a caravan-city on the River Euphrates on the border of the Roman and Parthian Empires. In 1868 it was discovered scratched on the wall of a 3rd Century Roman house at Cirencester, near Gloucester.*

📖 *The discovery in Deansgate, Manchester, places Christians there (180-190AD) less than 100 years after St John's Gospel was written (about 95AD). It is also significant that the vase points to the presence of Christians in northern England over 100 years before the death of the country's earliest Christian martyr, St Alban, about 305AD (which, in turn, was nearly 300 years before the arrival of St Augustine in 597).*

📖 *With it being illegal in the Roman Empire of that time to be a Christian, it could be useful having secret signs such as this which would only be recognisable by other Christians. People who were not Christian would simply see it as an amusing word-square whose words could be read in different directions.*

🎵 Follow me; For to those who love God;
   O Lord, all the world

AUGUST 2

1 Alexander Graham Bell was born in Edinburgh in 1819. He is now perhaps best remembered for having invented the telephone. He died in Canada on this day in 1922.

2 When he was aged 11, his friend's father saw Alexander and his own son playing around his water mill where farmers went to grind their corn. They were a distraction, and he asked if they could find something useful to do. He handed them some wheat and asked them to take the husks off the head of wheat. They set to experimenting and, later in life, Bell would look back on this moment as the time when he began to be creative and invent.

3 Alexander's two brothers died of tuberculosis (T.B.). His parents, anxious not to lose their remaining son, sent him to Canada, away from the dampness of Scotland. A year later his health improved and he moved south to the United States, teaching in the Boston School for the Deaf. He was particularly keen to invent something that might change the sound of a person talking into something that somehow could be seen by deaf people. As it happened, his experimenting led him to invent the telephone.

4 Alexander worked with people who had problems with speech and hearing, as also did his father and grandfather. His mother was almost completely deaf. He grew up with a sensitivity towards people with difficulties, and he knew that people tended to take their senses for granted until they were lost. He wrote these words:

5 *"We are all too much inclined, I think,*
to walk through life
with our eyes closed.
There are things around us
and right at our very feet
that we have never seen
because we have never really looked."

6 *Let us pray:*

Lord our God, open us up
to your Spirit living within us,
that we may live fully
each day of our lives.
Touch us,
that we may become more aware
of all that is around us,
growing in a sense
of wonder and awe,
and in appreciation
for all that we see and hear
and touch and taste and smell.
May we live in such a way
that we never
take anything for granted,
but always be appreciative
and express our thanks
to those who are part of our lives.
Amen.

❖❖❖❖❖❖❖❖❖❖❖❖❖❖❖❖❖

📖 See also 10 March for Alexander Graham Bell (3/3/1847-2/8/1926). He was a friend of the deaf and blind Helen Keller. For similar themes see 'Helen Keller' - 1st and 3rd June.

📖 Bell also invented a wax cylinder to record sound, being an early form of record-player. He invented the audiometer, used to detect the particular problem a person may have with hearing. He helped develop the aileron (the moving part of an aeroplane wing) and an early form of a hydrofoil boat. He was one of the founders of the National Geographic Society.

📖 Isaiah 35 - a reading used in Advent, including: "Then the eyes of the blind shall be opened, and the ears of the deaf unsealed" (verse 5).

🎵 Amazing grace; Christ is our king; If I am lacking love; I give my hands; Lay your hands

3 AUGUST

1 The *'Guinness Book of Records'* lists Jeanne Calment as the world's oldest person. Her birth certificate confirmed her age. Tomorrow, 4th August, commemorates her death in 1997, 5 months after marking her 122nd birthday.

2 To put her age into context, she was born in 1887. At that time, most of the world's modern inventions were undiscovered - including the radio and telephone. When she was 13 she met the artist, Vincent Van Gogh, as he shopped at her father's art store. When she was aged 14, Queen Victoria died. She rode a bicycle until she was 100, and used to remark that a smile was her recipe for long life.

3 When Jeanne Calment was aged 90, a local lawyer (aged 47) asked to buy her flat. They signed a contract that he would pay her a certain amount of money each year, and then he would inherit her flat when she died. As she was then aged 90, the lawyer didn't expect her to live long - and certainly not to the age of 122!

4 As the arrangement had been that the lawyer would pay her a certain amount each year, he ended up giving her a total of £100,000 - three times the actual value of the house - and then **he** died before she did!

5 *Let us pray for ourselves, that we may live fully and peacefully each day of our lives - thinking, too, of those who are presently living the last few years of their lives:*

6 **Lord Jesus,**
> **we can think of your people**
> **down the ages**
> **who have travelled over**
> **life's stormy sea**
> **and, in dying,**
> **have reached the harbour**
> **of peace, light and happiness.**

As you calmed the sea,
> **we ask you to be with us**
> **and bring peace in our lives each day,**
> **because the boat of our own lives**
> **is small**
> **and the ocean is very large.**

As you have set our course,
> **we ask you to steer our lives**
> **towards the shore of everlasting life.**

Bring us, at last,
> **along with all who are dear to us,**
> **to the quiet rest that we seek,**
> **where you live and reign**
> **with the Father and the Holy Spirit,**
> **one God, for ever and ever. Amen.**

📖 Jeanne Calment's life spanned the governments of 20 French presidents. She described Van Gogh by saying that he was "as ugly as sin". See 16 May for Van Gogh.

📖 The reflection, "A smile costs nothing", can be found on 17 June.

📖 Poem: "When you are old" by W.B.Yeats

📖 "Jesus calming the sea" is found in Mark, chapter 4. See the meditation given as the second part of 21 August.

📖 Part of the prayer is based on one written by St Augustine.

♩ Abide with me; Be not afraid *("death is at your side")*; Be still and know I am with you; Do not be afraid; Father, I place; If God is for us *("I know that neither death nor life")*; In you, my God; Lord of all hopefulness

1 John Vianney was aged 3 when the French Revolution began. He became a shepherd-boy in his village near Lyons in southern France. When he was 28 years old he was ordained a priest.

2 People began to discover that he was a good and holy person. Many came to hear him preach and, particularly, to go to him for the Sacrament of Reconciliation. People from all over France came to visit him, and he would spend up to 18 hours a day hearing the confessions of people, sharing with them God's compassion and forgiveness. In his last year, over 100,000 pilgrims visited the small village of only 300 people.

3 It was on this day in 1859, that John Vianney died. As is the case with most saints, the date of his death is also his feastday, because the day of death is considered the person's "birth-day in heaven."

4 John Vianney said:

"We do not have to talk very much
in order to pray well.
We know that God is there...
Let us open our hearts to him.
Let us rejoice in his presence.
This is the best prayer."

5 Let's simply pause for a moment in silence in God's presence

(pause...)

"We do not have to talk very much
in order to pray well.
We know that God is there...
Let us open our hearts to him.
Let us rejoice in his presence.
This is the best prayer."

📖 The quote of John Vianney about prayer is one of a list of quotes treasured by Pope John XXIII. That list is printed as an appendix to Pope John's "Journal of a Soul".

📖 St John Vianney: 1786-1859. He said:
"It is always spring-time
in the heart that loves God."

📖 John Vianney is often known as the "Curé d'Ars" - the parish-priest of the remote village of Ars-en-Dombes in southern France. He is the patron saint of the secular clergy i.e. those who "belong" to a diocese (and so are not members of religious orders).

📖 See also 12 August re priesthood.

📖 It was on this day in 1944 that Anne Frank was arrested. See 12 March.

🎵 Be still and know I am with you; God forgave my sin; Lord Jesus Christ, you have come to us ("teach us how to pray"); Oh the love of my Lord; The love I have for you

5 AUGUST

1 3 years before the start of the Second World War, the Olympic Games were held in Berlin, the capital of Hitler's Germany. 53 nations were competing, and the Games were designed to show to the world how advanced, cultured and powerful Germany had become.

2 On the opening day, the first-ever German champion of any Olympics was Hans Woellke, having won in the shotput. Hitler insisted that the champion be paraded before him.

3 Strict racial laws had come into force in Germany. Just a few years from then, millions of Jews (amongst others) would be murdered. Meanwhile the Olympic team of the United States included Jews and coloured people. Hitler had called black people an "inferior race". Those same people dominated the sprints and hurdles and field events.

4 On this day, the star of those 1936 Olympics - Jesse Owens, a black American - won the 200 metre race in a record 20.7 seconds. Hitler was furious. Publicly he had congratulated other Olympic winners but, on seeing Jesse Owens win, Hitler immediately left the stadium. Hitler refused to acknowledge Jesse Owens - one of the world's greatest athletes - because he was black, an African American. Instead, Hitler congratulated privately the silver medallist, who was a German.

5 *Let us pray:*

**Lord, I pray for all who suffer
from hatred and prejudice,
from abuse and ill-treatment,
and for all who are victims
of what others do.
I pray, too, for the people of violence,
that they may change their ways
and learn to respect others.**

**I pray for myself,
that when I face
what is negative or evil
I may have
the courage and generosity
to break the cycle
of violence, hatred, fear or distrust,
and make my own choices
and take responsibility
for the direction
in which I want my life to go.
I pray that I may always do to others
as I would wish them to do to me.
Amen.**

🖎 *During the 1936 Berlin Olympics, Jesse Owens won 4 gold medals. He equalled the Olympic Record of 10.30 seconds for the 100 metre sprint. He gained new Olympic and World records of 20.7 seconds for the 200 metre sprint. He set a new Olympic Record with his long jump of 8.05 metres. He was one of the 4-man relay team of 4x100 metres, setting a new Olympic and World Record of 39.8 seconds.*

🖎 *Jesse Owens: 1913-1980.*

🖎 *Alternative prayers would be those of 29 January, 21 March (detailing Jesus' involvement with people from different nations), 27 June.*

♦ Though the mountains may fall *("run and never tire")*; Yahweh, I know *("Where can I run from your love?")*

AUGUST 6

1   On this day every year, thousands gather in Hiroshima, Japan. They meet for a prayer service in the Peace Memorial Park that is built on the site where the atomic bomb exploded in 1945.

2   The use of the bomb on the city of Hiroshima (and then on Nagasaki 3 days later) forced the Japanese to surrender and bring the Second World War to a close. All that had been seen of the way that the Japanese fought, led the Americans to conclude that every person would fight to the death - civilians as well as soldiers. The taking of each island occupied by the Japanese would cost so many lives on both sides and lengthen the war considerably, that it was argued that use should be made of the atomic bomb to bring the war to a swift end.

3   The single bomb is thought to have killed about 140,000 people in Hiroshima at that time. The heat blast from the bomb flattened more than 10 square kilometres (4 square miles) of the city. People 2$^1/_2$ miles away suffered severe burning. Many died in later years from the effects of radiation.

4   Let's pray in silence for all victims of war and violence and unrest in our own times.

(pause...)

📖 At about 8.15 on the morning of 6th August, the bomb (named "Little Boy") was dropped by a B-29 bomber called the "Enola Gay". It detonated about 550m above the ground. There are now bombs that are almost 1,000 times as powerful as that dropped on Hiroshima.

📖 Today is also the feast of the Transfiguration (see Mt 17$^{1-8}$; Mk 9$^{2-8}$; Lk 9$^{28-36}$).
Pope Paul VI died on this day in 1978.

🎵 Come, let us go up to the Lord (sung slowly); Lord, make me a means; Make me a channel

125

7 AUGUST

1 The Apollo 15 spacecraft splashed down into the ocean on this day in 1971. The astronauts had spent 2 days 18 hours on the Moon. One of them, James Irwin, wrote that the greatest effect of that spaceflight had been to deepen and strengthen his faith and all the religious insight he ever had.

2 *"When you lean far back and look up, you can see the earth like a beautiful, fragile tree ornament against the blackness of space. It's as if you can reach out and hold it in your hand.*

3 *"As we reached out in a physical way to the heavens, we were moved spiritually. As we flew into space we had a new sense of ourselves, of the earth, and of the nearness of God. We were outside of ordinary reality; I sensed the beginning of some sort of deep change taking place inside me. Looking back at the spaceship we call "Earth", I was touched by a desire to convince mankind that we have a unique place to live, that we are unique creatures, and that we must learn to live with our neighbours.*

4 *"I had become a sceptic about getting guidance from God, and I know that I had lost the feeling of his nearness. On the moon, the total picture of the power of God and his Son, Jesus Christ, became abundantly clear to me."*

5 We'll use as our prayer today Psalm 8, a copy of which was left on the Moon in a metal canister during the first manned landing in July 1969:

6 *Let us pray:*

Lord, our God and King,
your greatness is seen
throughout the earth.

7 **When I gaze at the heavens**
which your fingers have formed,
and look at the moon and the stars
which you have set there,
I realise how small we are
in the magnificence of your creation.

8 **Yet you treasure us**
above all that you have made,
and you give us control
over all the works of your hand
- animals both wild and tame,
birds in the air,
and the creatures of the sea.

9 **Lord, our God and King,**
your greatness is seen
throughout the earth.

📖 *The quote is from Jim Irwin's book, 'To Rule the Night'.*

🎼 I watch the sunrise *("moonlight")*; O Lord my God, the Father of creation; O Lord my God, when I in awesome wonder

1 Every child of the Jewish faith learns the words of a prayer called the *"Shema".* Its opening words are these:

> *"Hear, Israel, and listen:*
> *the Lord our God is the only God.*
> *You shall love the Lord your God*
> *with all your heart,*
> *with all your soul,*
> *and with all your strength."*

2 Each morning and evening Jews recite these and some other words from the Bible that together make up the *"Shema"*, which is Hebrew for *"hear"* or *"listen"*, the first word of the prayer. The same passage continues:

> *"Let these words today*
> *be written in your heart.*
> *Write them, too,*
> *on the doorposts of your house."*

3 And so Jewish families have a small, thin container made of wood or metal attached to the right-hand doorpost of their homes. This prayer box, called a *"Mezuzah"* is a few centimetres long and maybe a centimetre wide. It contains some parchment on which is written the words of the *"Shema"*. As family members enter the house, they touch the *"Mezuzah"* as a sign of respect for God and for what he has told them to do. It also serves as a reminder of God's presence.

4 The opening words - *"the Lord our God is the only God"* - were first spoken to the people of Israel when they were led out from slavery in Egypt and guided towards the Promised Land. Down the ages Jews have held firmly to their belief in one God, giving priority in their lives only to him.

5 *Let us pray:*

Lord, inspire me
to get my priorities right
and make my choices wisely.
Amen.

📖 The "Shema" consists of the following verses:
Deut 6$^{4\text{-}9}$: (as mentioned)
Deut 11$^{13\text{-}21}$: If you obey God, you and your children will live long in the land I give you.
Numbers 15$^{37\text{-}41}$: Put tassels on your garments to remind you of my commandments. I brought you out of the land of Egypt so that I may be your God.

📖 *Over many centuries the daily recitation of the "Shema" has served as a personal and collective statement of belief (a kind of "creed"), rejecting the worship of various gods of the oppressive forces of the empires of Egypt, Babylon and Rome, as well as the evil that the Jewish people encountered in the 20th Century. Contrast today's reflection with that of 9th August.*

📖 Judaism's belief in ONE God became the basis, too, for Christianity and Islam. The three are called the world's "mono-theistic" religions - a word that means "one God".

📖 *We can recall how Jesus was asked which was the greatest commandment of all. He replied by quoting the opening words of the "Shema" - see Mark 12$^{28\text{-}34}$, and a different approach appears in Matthew 22$^{34\text{-}40}$.*

🎼 Do not be afraid; If I am lacking love; Lord of all hopefulness; The Lord's my shepherd

9 AUGUST

(See also 31 May.)

1   The following words are on display in a public place. Many thousands of people have read them:
      "Obedience, honesty,
      order, cleanliness,
      truthfulness, sacrifice,
      and love of one's country."

2   They are fine qualities and values for a person to have and develop, and the words are intended to inspire the readers. Where are they written?

3   They form the inscription on the ceiling of one of the administration buildings in Dachau, the Nazi concentration camp, near Munich. Prisoners were to read these words frequently. It is good, of course, to develop such values as are listed, but there is something "twisted" and horrific when we remember where it is that these words are seen:

4   *"Obedience, honesty,*
      order, cleanliness,
      truthfulness, sacrifice,
      and love of one's country."

5   In silence I can try to imagine myself there as an inmate at Dachau, reading those words whilst thinking of what was going on in that terrible place. I can also try to think of what might encourage me there.

    (pause...)

✍ Contrast what is written for 8th August: Jewish people are reminded of their values and heritage when they touch the "mezuzah" beside their front door.

✍ Dachau is near Munich in Germany, about 50 km from the Austrian border. Over 2,000 priests were sent to Dachau.

1 Some libraries throughout Britain and the United States - especially small ones - bear some wording on the building: *"Funded by Carnegie".*

2 Tomorrow, 11th August, is the anniversary of the death in 1919 of Andrew Carnegie. He was born of a poor family in Scotland, and later emigrated to the United States, aged 13. There, in the State of Pennsylvania, he found work as a bobbin boy, replacing cotton bobbins in a mill, having to work 11 hours a day. Later he worked his way up in a telegraph office and with a railway company.

3 He had started with nothing, but became very wealthy in the Pullman Railway Company and by investing in land where there was coal, iron and oil. After the American Civil War he founded a company that produced iron railway bridges, and then he formed his own iron and steel corporation.

4 Although he had little education himself in school, he was always particularly interested in education and books. Whilst he was alive, Andrew Carnegie gave away more than $350 million to projects dealing with education, culture and peace. 1,700 libraries across the United States and Britain received money from him.

5 Andrew Carnegie said:
"The man who dies rich, dies disgraced."

We can pause to ask ourselves what he may have meant by those words.

(pause...)

6 *Let us pray:*

Lord Jesus,
you talked about the need for us
to have our priorities right,
and not to hoard possessions.

You said that where our treasure is,
there our heart and commitment
will really be.
Touch our hearts
that we may love people
and use things
- and never the other way around.
Inspire us to seek first your kingdom
and use our talents and gifts
for the benefit of others. **Amen.**

> *"The man who dies rich,*
> *dies disgraced."*

📖 *Andrew Carnegie built a great concert hall in New York City which bears his name, Carnegie Hall. He donated funds for the building of the Peace Palace in The Hague (the city which is the seat of government of Holland). The building is now the International Court of Justice of the United Nations.*

📖 *Luke 12[13-34] - "I will pull down my barns and build bigger ones", said the rich man... Jesus says: "Trust in providence and have treasure that will last. Where your treasure is, there will your heart be, too."*

📖 *See also 14 July.*

📖 "God created people to be loved.
and things to be used.
Whenever this order is reversed,
tragedy results."
                                    (Revel Howe)

🎵 All that I am; Do not worry; I give my hands; O Lord all the world; Seek ye first

11 AUGUST

1 Astronomers are able to predict with accuracy the dates and times of eclipses of the moon or the sun.

2 An eclipse of the sun is observed when part of the sun appears black. The moon has moved between the sun and the earth, blocking out at least some of the sun's light reaching the earth.

3 A total eclipse of the sun occurs when the moon completely blocks out the sun's light, and so that part of the earth is then completely in the moon's shadow.

4 At 12.10pm on this day in 1999 a 2-minute total eclipse of the sun was (will be) observed in west Cornwall. With Cornwall having more miles of road than any other county - but many of them small, narrow, winding country roads - the police prepared plans in advance to handle the thousands of extra vehicles in the area.

5 Britain's next total solar eclipse won't be until 2090. The previous total eclipse in Britain was in 1927 in northern England.

6 Let us pray:

Lord Jesus,
   you are the light of the world.
Let us never cut ourselves off
   either from the light and life
   that you give to us,
   or from the good influence
   that others have on us.
When we encounter darkness
   in our lives,
   enable us to bring to it
   the light that we already have
   within us.   Amen

✍ When it was announced in France in 1560 that an eclipse of the sun would occur, many people thought the end of the world was approaching. People panicked and began fighting with each other for a place in queues to see priests for 'Confession' (the Sacrament of Reconciliation).

✍ During a total eclipse of the sun ('solar eclipse', the outer part of the sun's atmosphere becomes visible. In normal circumstances the intense brightness of the sun itself prevents us from distinguishing the outer part, called the sun's 'corona'.

✍ The sun is 400 times wider than the moon, and happens to be 400 times further away from the earth than is the moon. This co-incidence results in the sun and the moon appearing to be the same "size" when viewed from the earth.

✍ An eclipse of the moon takes place when the reflected light from the moon is "cut off" because the moon travels into the shadow cast by the earth. The earth lies in-between the sun and the moon.

✍ There is a saying: "Be like the sundial that records only the light and goodness of the day."

✍ An alternative prayer would be that of 21 June.

♪ Colours of day ("the sun disappears"); I watch the sunrise; Only a shadow; The light of Christ

130

1 During his Visit to Britain in 1982, Pope John Paul II ordained some men as priests in Manchester. As we listen to the words he spoke, we can think of particular priests whom we know or have known:

2 *"You must be men of God,*
his close friends.
You must develop daily patterns of prayer,
and penance
must be a regular part of your life.
Prayer and penance will help you
to appreciate more deeply
that the strength of your ministry
is found in the Lord
and not in human resources…
You must try to deepen every day
your friendship with Christ.
You must also learn to share
the hopes and the joys,
the sorrows and the frustrations
of the people entrusted to your care…
When you celebrate the sacraments
at the decisive moments of their lives,
help them to trust
in Christ's promised mercy
and compassion."

3 *Let us pray for all priests whom we know:*

God our Father, we pray
   for those whom you have called
   to serve your people as priests.
Every day
   may they live in your presence
   and deepen their friendship
   with Jesus, your Son.
Fill them with your Spirit
   and inspire them
   to be faithful in prayer
   and always place their trust in you.
May they grow in faith and compassion
   as they celebrate
   the Sacraments of your love
   and bring good news to the poor
   and healing to the broken-hearted.

Inspire them to live in such a way
   that they are credible witnesses
   of the transforming power
   of your love,
   as they share the hopes and the joys,
   the sorrows and the frustrations
   of those entrusted to their care.
Give them the gifts they need
   to accompany your people
   along the path of holiness. Amen.

> *"Try to deepen every day*
> *your friendship with Christ."*

📖 *John Paul ordained these priests in Heaton Park, Manchester, on 31 May 1982.*

📖 *See also 4 August re priesthood.*

🎵 Do not worry ("*trust and pray*"); Lord Jesus Christ, you have come to us ("*teach us how to pray*"); O Lord all the world; Take my hands.

1 At the end of the Second World War, defeated Germany was occupied for several years by the armies of 4 countries - Britain, France, the Soviet Union, and the United States - each temporarily supervising an area. Although Berlin, the German capital, was situated within the Soviet Zone in the east, it was also divided into 4 zones.

2 Within a very short time, relationships deteriorated between the Americans, British and French on one side, and the Soviets on the other.

3 In 1948, the Soviet Zone of Germany decided to become a separate country - Communist "East Germany" - leaving the larger part as "West Germany".

4 The united zones of Berlin became known as "West Berlin", initially protected by the troops of Britain, France and the USA. West Berlin was completely surrounded by Communist East Germany.

5 From 1949 onwards, nearly 3 million people left East Germany - most by simply walking into West Berlin. The Communist countries felt they could no longer allow this to continue, especially as they were losing many of their skilled and professional people - 2,000 each day by 1961.

6 As people woke up on this day in 1961, they discovered that road blocks and miles of barbed wire had been set up to stop people walking into West Berlin. Within the next few days a 4-metre high cement wall was built, and armed sentries occupied watchtowers. The Berlin Wall was 29 miles (47 km) in length, surrounding West Berlin. The Berlin Wall was a symbol of the divisions and mistrust between the countries of the West and the Communist Bloc.

7 As Communism started to collapse in Eastern Europe in 1989, ordinary people began to demolish parts of the Berlin Wall, and Germany became united in October 1990.

8 *Let us pray:*

**Lord, if I ever cut people off
  or isolate myself
  from the needs of others,
  alert me to what I am doing.
Open my eyes
  to see what unites people
  rather than what divides us.
Show me
  how to build bridges
  between people
  rather than putting up walls
  that divide. Amen.**

❖❖❖❖❖❖❖❖❖❖❖❖❖❖❖❖❖❖

📖 *At least 70 people were killed between 1961 and 1989, attempting to cross into West Berlin. The Berlin Airlift (or Blockade) took place between June 1948 and May 1949 in response to the Soviet and East German authorities blocking all land routes to West Berlin.*

📖 *In the synoptic gospels (i.e. those that "look alike" - Matthew, Mark and Luke) we read that, at the time of Jesus' death, the veil of the Temple was torn in two. This was the curtain that divided the "Holy of Holies" of God's presence (the Ark of the Covenant) from the people. The sudden tearing of this curtain can be thought of as symbolising that God is now fully "available" to all people. The tearing of the curtain can be read about in Mt 27^{51}, Mk 15^{38}, and Lk 23^{45}.*

📖 *For an alternative prayer on injustice and freedom, see 24 March. See also Easter Sunday, volume 1.*

 Lord, make a means; Make me a channel

1 It was 1941, and one of the prisoners had escaped from Auschwitz, the Nazi Concentration Camp in southern Poland. The punishment on the whole camp was that ten other prisoners would die. The camp commandant walked up and down between rows of prisoners. The tenth man he selected was a Polish soldier. The sergeant broke down and begged for mercy because of his wife and young family who would have no support without him.

2 A thin figure moved forward, took off his cap, and asked if he might take that man's place in the death cell. "Who are you?" he was asked. "I am a Catholic priest," he replied. He was Prisoner 16670, Maximilian Kolbe, a Franciscan priest.

3 The exchange was agreed. Now that the group was 10 in number, they were marched off to Block 13 - the death-block. They were not to be shot or gassed. They were to die very slowly by being starved of even the very little food that the prisoners were normally given. Their very slow death was designed to put others off from trying to escape.

4 In the following days, the guards observed the condemned men dying slowly. They also saw that the men were gathered round Father Maximilian, laughing together, praying and singing hymns. One by one the men died - a slow death over 14 days. The last one alive was Maximilian Kolbe and, on this day - August 14th - in 1941, a guard injected him with phenol into his left arm. He died almost immediately.

5 The Polish sergeant - Franz Gajounicezek - survived Auschwitz and the war itself. Each year he visited that dreadful place and laid a wreath beside Block 13 where Maximilian Kolbe died instead of himself.

6 In 1982, 41 years after Maximilian Kolbe's death, Pope John Paul II canonised him - declared him to be a saint.

7 *Let us pray:*

Lord Jesus, you said
that no-one could have greater love
than to give up their life
for someone else.
Remind us
in our personal circumstances today
that care and compassion
and love and sacrifice
can change everything. Amen.

📖 Kolbe was aged 47 at his death. Fellow-Pole, John Paul II, canonised him on 10th October 1982. They had both lived in the town of Kracow in Poland and, at the time of Maximilian Kolbe's imprisonment, the future Pope was working in a stone quarry and a chemical factory whilst preparing to become a priest.

📖 Franz Gajounicezek later said: "At first I felt terrible that another man was dying in my place. But then I realised that he had done this not just to save my life, but to be with the other nine in their terrible agony of dying. His nearness to them in those dreadful last hours was worth more than a lifetime of preaching."

📖 Auschwitz is situated 20 miles outside the city of Krakow in Poland, near the Czech and Slovak borders. It was the largest concentration camp run by Nazi Germany. More than 1.5 million people were killed there. As that is too large a figure to begin to grasp, we might picture the same number of people as in 1,500 secondary schools that each have 1,000 students.

📖 John 15[13]: Jesus said: "No greater love can anyone have than to lay down their life for their friends."

🎵 All that I am; If God is for us *("neither death nor life can ever take us from his love")*; Take my hands

133

15 AUGUST

(See also 20 May)

1 Today is the Feast of what is called the "Assumption of the Blessed Virgin Mary into Heaven". We can think of this feastday as Jesus saying to Mary: *"Welcome home, Mother!"*

2 A story was written 800 years ago about a man who was a juggler and acrobat, who felt called to become a monk. He joined the monastery and prayed in his heart to God.

3 He wanted to pray with the other monks and join in the same words, but he found it very difficult because the Mass and other prayers at that time were spoken in Latin. It worried him that he wasn't able to join in the prayers. Did this mean that he couldn't pray? All he felt he could do was juggle and jump and turn somersaults and dance.

4 One day he discovered a small chapel in the crypt under the monastery church. There he could pray and no-one would see him. He was praying there silently one day at midday when he heard the monastery bell ring to summon the monks to pray together in the church above. The juggler remained where he was. He began to cry as he heard his brother-monks pray and sing together. Then he prayed before a statue of Our Lady: *"Holy Mary,"* he said *"pray for me now and always. All I can do is juggle and jump and turn somersaults and dance. What I have learned to do, I will now do well for you. Accept this now as my prayer before you."* And then he began to juggle and jump and turn somersaults and dance before the statue of the Virgin Mary, whilst the other monks prayed and sang in the way that **they** knew best in the church above.

5 Every day he prayed in this way in the small chapel at midday. The other monks knew that he went there each day, but he never spoke of what he did. One day another monk followed him, annoyed that he was not praying with the others. He hid behind a pillar. Then, as the monastery bell began to ring, our friend bowed before the statue representing the Virgin Mary and started to juggle and jump and turn somersaults and dance, and did so until he fell to the ground with exhaustion.

6 The monk who had followed, felt disturbed at what he had seen and went to tell the abbot (the head of the monastery) who swore him to tell no-one what had happened. The following day the abbot himself hid behind a pillar and watched as his brother-monk juggled and jumped and turned somersaults and danced before the image of the Virgin Mary. And, as the abbot looked, he saw Our Lady herself appear before the monk, and she took a cloth and began to fan the monk to cool him from the exhaustion of his juggling and jumping and turning somersaults and dancing. No-one more beautiful had the abbot ever seen, and he saw that the Lady had great concern and care for the monk who had prayed to her.

7 The following day the abbot asked to see the monk, who thought he was going to be criticised for not joining the other monks at their midday prayer. The abbot greeted the monk and set his mind at rest. *"Pray for me,"* said the abbot, *"and I, too, will pray for you. My dear friend, I have seen how you have prayed to Our Lady. Pray in this way in the monastery church with your brothers present, so that they may be blessed and see the holiness of your prayer."*

8 *And so we pray today:*

Mary, our Mother,
   your total giving of yourself
   reminds us
   that we hold in trust
   from God our Father
   all our accomplishments
   and talents and gifts
   - trusted as we are
   to offer them in his service,
   and bring happiness and well-being
   to our brothers and sisters.
Your "Yes" to God's invitation
   to be the mother of his Son
   reminds us
   that prayer is not just words
   but is from the heart.
We ask you to pray to Jesus for us
   that the Holy Spirit
   may live fully in us, too,
   so that we may pray
   in the way that each of us finds best.
So may we be prepared to join you
   in saying "Yes" to God our Father,
   that Jesus may be born anew
   in our hearts.
Amen.

📖 *This story, "Le Jongleur de Notre Dame", of one who joins the Cistercian monastery of Clairvaux near Dijon, in central France, is found in a collection made by Gautier de Coinci in the 13th Century.*

🎼 'Hail Mary' by Carey Landry (found in many hymn books but could be played on tape: either from the tape/CD *"I will not forget you"* by Carey Landry, or from *"Sorrowful Woman"* by Marilla Ness).

Also: As I kneel before you; Give me joy in my heart; Holy Virgin, by God's decree; Oh Mary, when our God chose you; Sing a simple song; The angel Gabriel

16 AUGUST

1 No-one likes rain during their summer holidays, but torrential rain was the experience of people on this day in 1952 in Lynmouth, a very picturesque small holiday resort on the north coast of Devon.

2 On the 15th August it had rained very heavily for hour after hour. The soil of the huge area of the moor called Exmoor could soak up only so much water - the rest had to flow downhill. Although vast amounts of water had already fallen, at about 8.30 in the evening there was a cloudburst. Down came more torrential rain.

3 23 centimetres (9 inches) of rain fell in 24 hours, whereas the area normally received about 83 centimetres (33 inches) in a whole year! And so the river that, in a normal summertime, flowed from the moor over rocks and big boulders, now became a killer. Suddenly giant waves of water swept off the moor and picked up huge boulders and rocks as though they were tiny pebbles. The water and boulders and soil swept through the village of Lynmouth, destroying 28 bridges as though they were twigs. As electricity had been cut off, the people could not even see the tragedy that was upon them. Many buildings were destroyed or badly damaged. More importantly, 31 people were killed, and some of the bodies were never recovered. They were either lost under thick mud, or were washed out to sea. In the daylight of the morning of the 16th of August, the emergency services discovered how severe the tragedy was.

4 Lynmouth was a severe "natural disaster" in a country that doesn't normally have such experiences. Documentary TV programmes on natural disasters often include scenes of Lynmouth. Camera shots of the great size of the boulders of rock and the distance they were moved by the onrush of water, illustrate how powerful and destructive water can be.

5 *Let us pray:*

God our Father,
we have been reminded
of the destruction and even death
that water can bring,
and we can reflect
that we are called
to die to selfishness and sin
- living, instead,
in the fullness of life
that Jesus promises.
In a country that is blessed
with an abundance of water,
perhaps we don't fully appreciate
how vital water is for all life.
Water is used as a sign in Baptism
- a symbol of dying
to selfishness and sin,
and living the new life
that Jesus brings.
When Jesus was baptised
in the River Jordan,
he was placing himself beside
all who had sinned
and needed to make a new start
and live in a better way.
At that time, Father,
you were heard to say
that Jesus was your well-loved Son,
and the Holy Spirit rested upon him.
Fill us with your Spirit
that we may grow
in the realisation and faith
that we, too,
are your sons and daughters
whom you love greatly.
Amen.

📖 *Mt 7²⁴⁻²⁷ - Jesus said:* "Those who listen to what I say and really put my words into effect are like the sensible person whose house is built on rock. A gale blew against that house, and heavy rain fell and floods hit the house, but it did not fall. But people who don't dig deep in their life, who don't base their lives on my word, they are like those whose house is built only on sand. When the troubles of life hit those people, down come their houses. Prepare yourself well for life, and make strong foundations so that when troubles reach you, you will be able to withstand them."

📖 *The word "baptism" is from Greek, meaning to "immerse" or "dip".*

🎼 Oh living water; O let all who thirst

17 AUGUST

1 When Pope John Paul II visited Britain in 1982 he focussed on each of the Sacraments in turn. During his visit to York, couples were invited to renew their marriage vows. We'll base our prayer today on themes in his sermon at that time:

2 Let us pray for people who are married, that they may make choices to live sincerely and in compassion, in gentleness and patience, bearing with one another and forgiving one another. In these ways may their relationships grow and develop, and so may they remain faithful to each other in good times and bad.

Lord, in your mercy - *hear our prayer*.

3 Marriage is a sign of God's faithful and unbroken love. Let us pray that families may share in God's love, and grow as communities where young people are guided to maturity.

Lord, in your mercy - *hear our prayer*.

4 Let us pray that families may be generous in extending their love to lonely and burdened people locally, and to those who are on the margins of society.

Lord, in your mercy - *hear our prayer*.

5 We pray for those who know the pain of failure in marriage. We pray for those who know the loneliness of bringing up a family on their own. We pray for those whose family life is dominated by tragedy, or by illness of mind or body.

Lord, in your mercy - *hear our prayer*.

6 We see many damaged relationships around us. We ask for the gift of being able to build bridges between people.

Lord, in your mercy - *hear our prayer*.

📖 *This visit took place on 31/5/82 at Knavesmire Racecourse, York.*

📖 *The first prayer is based on Col 3^{12-14}, which John Paul incorporated in his sermon.*

📖 *The song "Endless love" by Diana Ross and Lionel Richie was the top single requested to be played at weddings during 1997, followed by Elton John's "Your Song", and then Bryan Adams' "Everything I do (I do it for you)", which was the theme tune of Kevin Costner's "Robin Hood, Prince of Thieves". It is a true story that one couple asked the organist in advance to play "that tune from Robin Hood" as the wedding procession was to leave the church. The elderly organist (who was a little puzzled by the request) amused everyone by playing the theme tune of the 1960s TV series of Robin Hood: "Robin Hood, Robin Hood, riding through the glen" !*

🎵 Father, I place; If I am lacking love; Love is his word; Peace, perfect peace; This is what Yahweh asks of you; This, then, is my prayer

1 Hitler's scientists set out to develop weapons that might bring the Second World War to a successful conclusion for Germany. "Intelligence" reports confirmed that a new terror weapon (later called the "V-1 flying bomb") was being produced at a weapons' base on the Baltic coast called Peenemünde. The night of 17th/18th August 1943 saw the bombing of Peenemünde by the Royal Air Force, which set back production of those terror weapons by several months.

2 The "V-1" was a pilotless flying bomb in the shape of an aeroplane. It needed a long ramp from which to be launched, and then flew at 370 miles per hour. The V-1 used the first jet engines, and carried a calculated amount of fuel such that they would fall and explode on London. They were called *"doodlebugs"* or *"buzz-bombs"* by Londoners. People felt safe as long as they could still hear the distinctive noise of the plane. When the noise suddenly stopped, everyone knew that the plane with its explosives would quickly hit the ground.

3 Films of the time show some of the V-1s being destroyed by anti-aircraft guns from the ground, or by bullets from aeroplanes, or even by having their wings tipped over by the RAF planes, causing them to crash and explode in unpopulated areas.

4 The V-weapons were named after the German word for "vengeance". The "V-2" was even more deadly than the "V-1", and did not need ramps to launch it. It was a long-range 14 metre (47 foot) long rocket, with a one-tonne warhead, hitting its target at 3,000 m.p.h (5,000 k.p.h.). Travelling faster than sound, the rockets were not heard before landing.

5 *Let us pray:*

God our Father,
  we read of the commandment
"do not kill"
  and think it doesn't apply to us
  because we don't take anyone's life.
Yet there are times
  when we take life from others
  by cruel words, sarcasm,
  doing people down,
  and gossiping.
Lead us to choose to bring life to others
  - and not death.
Inspire us to break the cycle
  of whatever is negative
  or violent or evil
  whenever we encounter them.
Let us not look for vengeance
  - to get our own back -
  but lead us to be generous
  and ready to conquer evil
  with goodness. Amen.

✍ "V" is an abbreviation of the German word "vergeltungswaffe" - "vengeance/reprisal weapons". Regarding "vengeance" (getting one's own back in a ruthless way) a Buddhist phrase records that
"hatred is never diminished by hatred.
Hatred is diminished by love.
This is the eternal law."

✍ The first V-1 was launched on England in the early morning of 13 June 1944. By September of that year the Allies had captured about 300 sites in northern France from which the V-1s were launched from ramps.

✍ The "V-2" was fuelled by ethanol burning with liquid oxygen. Both the V-1 and the V-2 were produced at Peenemünde. Fortunately the Germans could only produce small numbers of the V-2 rockets. A V-2 landed on London on 27 March 1945, being the last of some 1,115 launched against England which, in total, killed some 2,700 people, but brought fear and terror to very many more. Almost twice the number of V-2s that landed on London were fired on the Belgian cities of Brussels, Liège, and especially on the Port of Antwerp, to prevent the Allies using the port facilities of the city they had captured from the Germans.

✍ V-2 rockets captured by both the USA and the USSR became the basis for the Arms Race between those two countries, as well as their Space Programmes. The V-2 rocket was designed by the German engineer Wernher Von Braun, who was then taken to the United States where he helped develop the USA's NASA Space Programme.

✍ "Do not kill" - Ex 20^{13} ; Deut 5^{17}
"Choose life and not death" - Deut 30^{19}
"Conquer evil with goodness" - Rom 12^{21}

🎼 Come let us go up; Lord, make a means;
Make me a channel

1 Frank Baum was a newspaperman who put his writing talents to use in a series of children's books about a fairyland called the Land of Oz. His characters had wonderful adventures.

2 Frank Baum later adapted his book into a musical. 20 years after his death, a musical film called *"The Wonderful Wizard of Oz"* had its première yesterday (18th August) in 1939.

3 In the story there are four unhappy characters:

- a scarecrow who thinks he has no brain;

- a tin woodsman who thinks he has no heart;

- a lion who thinks he has no courage,

- and a girl called Dorothy who thinks she has no power to change anything in her life.

4 These four characters - all thinking little of themselves - believe that if they reach the Wizard of Oz he will change them so that they have the qualities and talents they would like. What they discover is that the Wizard doesn't force people to change; instead he cares about them. He sends each of them an invitation to see in themselves what they had not seen before.

5 And so the scarecrow discovers that he already does have a brain. The tin woodsman realises that he does already have a heart. The lion possesses all he needs to be courageous. Dorothy has what it takes to change things in her own life.

6 When Dorothy returns to Kansas (from where she had been taken by a tornado) she says to her aunt:
*"Oh, Aunt Em, I've been
to many strange and marvellous places,
looking for something*

*that was right here all along...
right in my own back yard!"*

7 *Let us pray:*

**God our Father, in saying
that you have written our names
on the palm of your hands,
you are telling us that each person
is unique and special to you.
We pray that individuals
may discover in themselves
the treasures you have given them,
and develop and put to good use
the qualities
they hold in trust from you.
I pray and commit myself today
to promote goodness and happiness,
by treating others
with respect
and care and understanding.
May others treat me today, Father,
in the same way as I treat them,
and so may we all
bring out the best in one another
and grow in the way
we look at ourselves and others.
Amen.**

📖 *Frank Lyman Baum: 1856-1919.*

📖 *Judy Garland starred as Dorothy in "The Wonderful Wizard of Oz", and sang "Over the rainbow".*

📖 *Could use the New Testament passage printed for 22 February (Philippians 4) about focussing on everything that is true and noble, good and pure, virtuous and worthy of praise.*

🎵 Do not worry; Follow me; I will never forget you

20 AUGUST

1 Two years running, Tom Hanks received the Oscar for "Best Actor" - in 1993 for his role in *"Philadelphia"*, and in 1994 for *"Forrest Gump"*. A line that he repeats as Forrest Gump is to say that *"life is like a box of chocolates."*

2 I can focus on "Quality Street" chocolates as I think of my own character.

3 The **green triangle** of chocolate. On the seashore we never see pebbles of this shape because, of course, any sharp edges are knocked off by others in the sea. Do I have any sharp edges to my character - do I get at people, annoy them? Do I make fun of others? Yet still there is good in the person that this might represent. This is good solid chocolate, but I need to knock off some of my sharp edges.

4 Those edges - the negative things - tend to be knocked off when I really share my life with others, as we see in the **round toffee cup**. I become more WHOLE as a person, more rounded in character, keeping life in balance, living life peacefully one day at a time.

5 **Fudge** - the paper comes off quietly, so this is the one to take if you're trying to sneak an extra one out of the box when no-one's looking! As there is a lot of sugar in fudge, so this individual has great richness within - a lot to offer others. People are the richer for having been with this person - the one who always smiles and forgives; the person who often speaks a word of encouragement and support; the one who is generous in doing something they'd rather not do. These people will make the world a better place for having walked in it.

6 Maybe I am a little like this one - the **purple hazelnut in caramel** - a little

showy, flashy on the outside. I have *two* wrappings - maybe to protect or hide my real self. Maybe I don't want anyone to know what I am really like deep inside - because, deep within... here is a nut!

7 The **green coconut**. 10 minutes after eating this, you find little bits of coconut between your teeth - something more to chew over. Maybe I am like this coconut - a challenging person because I leave things for others to think about, to "chew over". These people leave a little of themselves wherever they go: that compliment that really encourages someone; passing the joy of a contagious smile to another.

8 *Strawberry*. I might appear quite firm on the outside, perhaps giving the impression that I'm a little difficult to know at first, maybe rather shy. Inside there's something very special: a quiet person who gets on with life peacefully; a gentle character, happy with who I am; a person who quietly brings support and healing to those who are hurt; one who shows others how special they are.

9 *Orange*. This melts in your mouth if you let it, *but* some people find dark chocolate a little sickly, too. But why am I saying "BUT"? If I set out to look for negative things in others, I will find them. If I "LOOK" for the good - the quality - in other people, then I will come to see so much good around me. That "WAY OF LOOKING" (which should mark out a Christian school) - that "way of seeing" - will affect my whole life. Setting out each morning to look for the good in others will bring peace in my heart and a smile on my face throughout the day!

10 The **brown caramel**. This is the one you find in your pocket a week after putting it there! It's been squashed a bit, but it

doesn't go "gooey" in the pocket. It is firm: a solid character, faithful, trusting, accepting others for who they are, a true friend through good times and bad. It's a great compliment to be told that you are a friend on whom others can rely.

11 Maybe I am one of these **yellow cara-mels** - normally left to the last in our house. Do I sometimes feel a bit left out of things, feel that I'm not as popular as others? The last one to be chosen for something? And yet Jesus said that the way of **his** Kingdom is that *"the first will be last"*; that the 'insignigicant ones' are the important ones - the sparrows, the sinner, the lost coin, and Zacchaeus (the tax-collector whom people thought little but who was great, and walked tall in God's eyes). And even if I don't think too much of myself, there is One who tells me that he *"has written my name on the palm of his hands"*, as though I am the only one that exists.

12 Quality Street are all *different*: they would not be Quality Street if they were all the same. And when I come to meet the Maker of all this QUALITY, he will *not* ask me: "Why weren't you Mother Teresa?" He *will* be asking me if I have grown as the person he called me to be. In Christian schools we are not called to try to make people into something that they are not, but to invite people to be and to grow as who they already are.

13 Let us *be* people of quality! Let us do the ordinary things of life in an extraordinary way! We hope to see a street-cleaner collecting rubbish in the same committed way that Shakespeare wrote poetry! Let us make extraordinary use of our ordinary talents, because we are all called to be FULLY ALIVE, to be saints of God.

14 **And so we thank you, Lord,
for making us people of quality.
We pray that we may use our gifts well
and not keep them unused,
unwrapped,
because a gift is no good
unless it is shared.
We thank you
that we are people of quality
whom your hands have made.
May you be blessed forever!**

❖-❖-❖-❖-❖-❖-❖-❖-❖-❖-❖-❖-❖-❖-❖

📖 "the first will be last" - Mt 20^{16}
- sparrows - Mt 10$^{28-31}$
- 'lost' parables - Lk 15
- Zacchaeus - Lk 19$^{1-10}$
- name written on the palm of my hands
- Isaiah 49$^{15-16}$

Father, I place into your hands; I will never forget you

21 AUGUST

1 On this day in 1996 a replica of Shakespeare's Globe Theatre was opened in London on the south bank of the Thames, near where the original theatre was located 400 years before. The rebuilding of Shakespeare's octagonal open-air theatre was the vision of the American actor and film producer, Sam Wanamaker.

2 The new theatre is as exact a replica as possible of the original theatre of Shakespeare's day. Tudor building techniques have been followed, and the theatre is topped by the first thatched roof to be built in London since they were banned after the Great Fire of London in 1666.

3 No microphones or other electronic equipment are used in the new theatre, although floodlights are used at night to mimic daylight. The theatre remains open to the sky. People may sit in the three tiers of galleries that make the octagonal theatre, but many stand in front of the stage. As in the original building, members of the audience are free to move around during a production, and even eat and talk and heckle the actors. "Audience participation" is encouraged.

4 During the building work, it was said of the new theatre that it is
"built for the simple function of telling a story - we are all part of the story."

5 In that same way of becoming part of the story, of participating, we are invited to participate in the Gospel by becoming part of whatever event we are reading. Let's reflect on the Gospel account of Jesus calming the storm.

6 I imagine myself in the boat with Jesus and other close friends of his, as a storm brews up on the inland Sea of Galilee.

7 The day has been warm. I can still smell the salt water as well as the lingering odour of fish that have lain in the boat. I hear the birds that are disturbed by the sudden storm, and I see them fly off to the security of the land. I can feel the wind in my hair and the rain on my face. I see the white-topped waves as the wind scurries down the valleys that surround the Lake. I feel the disturbed, unsettling motion of the boat as the storm begins to toss it around, and I hear the waves smash against the side of the wooden boat. The sail makes a loud noise as the strong circulating wind makes it flap back and forth.

8 Now the rain drives harder and I hear the large drops strike the inside of the boat. What is normally a still and peaceful lake has become very disturbed and agitated. This is beyond my normal experience, and I know only too well that I am a poor swimmer, and the water here is deep.

9 The storm around me reminds me of the storm within - the confusion and worries, the doubts and fears in my own life. As I look around, I see the faces of those who have become my friends. My fear is reflected in the anxiety shown in their wet and worried faces.

10 Then I am surprised when I see that another figure - it is Jesus - not only is not bothered by the storm, but is actually asleep in the turbulent boat - and he even has his head on a cushion! I lean over and shake him to wake him up. He gives me that usual smile of his and looks directly into my eyes. I am surprised - but I think I'm also angry, and I say to him: *"Master, don't you care that we might sink?"* But then I realise it was a stupid thing to say, because I have often seen

his personal care for individuals. Now I see him stretch out his hand and command the wind and the waves to be still - and so they become. I feel that tingling down my spine that I always feel whenever something extraordinary happens. I look around and see the same puzzled - and perhaps fearful - expression on the faces of my friends. Again, Jesus smiles and looks at each one in turn, and then he says: *"Don't be afraid. What do you want me to do for you?"* And I pause in silence for a while, thinking over those words he has just spoken: *"Don't be afraid. What do you want me to do for you?"...*

(pause...)

✍ *Sam Wanamaker died in 1993, three years before the completion of his project, but it was carried on by his daughter, actor Zoe Wanamaker (who appeared in the 'Prime Suspect' series).*

✍ *Many of the plays of William Shakespeare (1564-1616) were performed in the original Globe Theatre by Richard Burbage and his company who had built the theatre in 1599. William Shakespeare was one of the shareholders. The theatre's roof bore a globe (giving the building its name), reflecting the quotation (in Latin) that was carved into the wood over the front of the theatre, stating that* "all the world's a stage" *(which may have been a quote of Petronius, who died in AD65). These words are incorporated in Shakespeare's 'As You Like It' (Act 2, Scene 7, line 139), adding:* "And all the men and women merely players." *Another reference is to be found in 'The Merchant of Venice' (Act 1, Scene 1, line 77).*

✍ *The theatre was accidentally burned down in 1613 by a cannon that was fired during a performance of Shakespeare's 'Henry VIII', setting light to the thatched roof. It was re-built the following year, but was destroyed by the Puritans in 1614. (See 26 February regarding the Great Fire of London of 1666).*

✍ *The Sea of Galilee is variously called Lake Tiberius or the Lake of Gennesaret or the Sea of Chinneroth.*

✍ *Although the meditation is based on the 'Calming of the Storm' in Mark 4^{35-41}, the final words in the meditation -* "What do you want me to do for you?" *- are not found in that passage, but in Mk 10^{51}.*

♪ I will be with you *("stormy waters")*; Walk with me, O my Lord *("just as you calmed the wind... conquer, my living Lord, the storms that threaten me" - verse 3)*

1 On the night of the 22nd August in 1741 a bent figure - looking older than his years - was seen to be moving slowly and unsurely along a dimly-lit street in London. The man was ill and depressed and was struggling with his life, especially as he had suffered a stroke a few years before, paralysing his right side, affecting his walking and writing.

2 This was the great composer George Frideric Handel, who was the king's chief musician. Feeling in despair he heard some words as he passed a church: *"My God, my God, why have you forsaken me?"*. These words of a psalm touched him deeply. He returned home and began to write some music. From this day, August 22nd, until September 14th he wrote his music almost non-stop, sleeping and eating little. What he wrote is now world-famous and is called *"The Messiah"*. On finishing this masterpiece, he slept for 17 hours. *"The Messiah"* is an opera in which singers present the life of Jesus from his birth to his death and resurrection, and so the music of Handel's *"Messiah"* is often sung, especially at Christmas and Easter.

3 When King George II attended a performance of Handel's *"Messiah"* he was so impressed and touched by the *"Hallelujah Chorus"* that he stood up. The audience saw the king and felt that if he stood up, then they should, too. In every performance, now, of Handel's *"Messiah"*, all the audience stand up throughout the *"Hallelujah Chorus"*.

4 Handel was a committed Christian, and all performances of his music whilst he was alive were in aid of charities of his choice. The *"Messiah"* was first performed in Dublin, in aid of some charities which included "poor and distressed people who were in prison for debt". Whilst talking about the time he was composing the *"Hallelujah Chorus"*, Handel is reputed to have said:
    "I thought I saw all heaven before me, and the great God himself."

5 Handel was completely blind for the last 6 years of his life. He died in London in 1759, and the last musical performance he heard was a week earlier, and it was his *"Messiah"*.

6 *Let us pray:*

   God our Father,
   I thank you
   that many people
   have used their gifts well
   and have helped me and inspired me
   and brought cheerfulness and joy
   in my life.
   May I, too,
   live in such a way
   that I bring blessings to others
   by my attitude and actions
   and my presence with them.
   Remain with me
   and lead me to that final day
   when I, too, will be able to say:
   "I see all heaven before me
   and the great God himself."
   Amen.

George Frideric Handel: 23/2/1685-14/4/1759. Aged 25, Handel worked for a few months in Hanover, Germany, and then moved to England. The Elector of Hanover (his former employer) became King George I of Great Britain in 1714, and so Handel became the music master to the king's children in London. In 1727 he took out British citizenship, settling on the spelling of "Handel" as his surname in the Act of Naturalisation as a British subject. Previously he had also spelt his name as Händel, Haendel and Hendel. Music that he wrote for State occasions includes his "Water Music" in 1717, and "Music for the Royal Fireworks" in 1749. He wrote four anthems for the coronation of George II, including the moving "Zadok the Priest", which is still used at the coronation ceremony of British kings and queens.

"My God, my God, why have you forsaken me?" is the first line of Psalm 21/22 which ends more optimistically - quoted by Jesus on the cross (Mk 15³⁴).

Abba, abba Father, you are the potter;
In you, my God; This, then, is my prayer

23 AUGUST

1 On many a Sunday at the back of Catholic churches will be someone collecting money for the "S.V.P." - the St Vincent de Paul Society. They are a group of people found in most parishes who volunteer to be of help to local people who are in need.

2 There are a million members of the S.V.P. world-wide, helping the poor locally. Over 18,000 volunteers in Britain make more than a million and a half visits each year to needy people in their homes, as well as in hospital and prisons. Special projects include holidays for the needy, charity shops, day centres and hostels for the homeless, the mentally ill and for young people at risk. They provide hostels for those on probation or bail, and also offer support to refugees, unemployed people, and those with drug or alcohol problems. The S.V.P. Society also has set up a housing association.

3 It was a Frenchman, Frédéric Ozanam, who founded the SVP Society. On this day in 1997 Pope John Paul II beatified him - naming him "Blessed Frédéric Ozanam", being a step on the way to calling him a saint. Saints are people put forward as an example from whom we can learn. Frédéric was a married man living with great faith and concern for other people. He wrote that he
"dreamed of encircling the whole world with a network of love and care."

4 *Let us pray:*

> **Lord, may my attitude**
> **and all that I think and do**
> **always be based on**
> **a spirit of love and care,**
> **so that I may make a difference**
> **in my own part of the world**
> **by treating people**
> **as individuals. Amen.**

📖 *It was on World Youth Day, 22nd August 1997, during his visit to France that Pope John Paul II beatified Frédéric Ozanam in the Cathedral of Notre Dame in Paris.*

📖 *Frédéric Ozanam founded the SVP Society in 1833, and modelled it on St Vincent de Paul's life and ministry. Vincent de Paul had founded a religious order of Sisters: the Daughters of Charity. Vincent de Paul died in 1660 and is now the patron saint of all charitable societies.*

📖 *Ozanam's writings and ministry helped to inspire the preparation of the landmark papal encyclical 'Rerum Novarum' in 1891 by Pope Leo XIII. Frédéric Ozanam (who died in 1853, aged only 40) wrote:*
"There is exploitation of person by person when the owner treats the worker not as an associate or helper, but as a means by which he can get the greatest work done whilst paying the lowest possible wage."

📖 *He also wrote:*
"The question which divides people today is whether society will be merely an immense exploitation for the benefit of the strongest, or a consecration of everyone for the service of all. There are many people who own too much and want to have even more; there are many others who have nothing and want to grab if they are not given anything. A struggle between these two groups is threatening and will be terrible: on one side the power of gold, and on the other the might of despair."

📖 *See also 18 March for similar ideas regarding work, which quotes from 'The Common Good' a pivotal document on social issues produced in 1996 by The Catholic Bishops of England and Wales.*

🎼 All that I am; God's Spirit is in my heart;
I give my hands

AUGUST 24

1 In 1933, an attempt was made to climb the world's highest mountain, Mount Everest, by F.S.Smythe. His fellow-climber could go no further, so he decided to go on a little way by himself. Smythe writes of what happened when he tried to climb alone:

2 *"After leaving Eric, a strange feeling possessed me that I was accompanied by another. This 'presence' was strong and friendly. In its company I could not feel lonely, neither could I come to any harm. It was always there to sustain me in my solitary climb up the snow-covered slabs. As I halted and extracted some mint-cake from my pocket, it was so near and so strong that I instinctively divided the mint into two halves and turned round with one half in my hand to offer it to my 'companion'."*

3 Let's pause for a moment to remind ourselves that we are in the presence of God...

(pause...)

4 *Let us pray:*

> **Lord Jesus,**
> **open my eyes to recognise you**
> **as you walk beside me,**
> **accompanying me**
> **on my journey in life each day.**
> **Amen.**

🕮 *The quote is from 'Camp Six' by F.S.Smythe: Hodder and Stoughton. Smythe did not succeed in reaching the top of Everest. That victory would not come for another 20 years, and that would be by Edmund Hillary and Tenzing Norkay - see 29 May.*

🕮 *The next highest mountain is also in the Himalayas, and is called "K2", which is 240 metres lower than Mount Everest. On 16th May 1975 Junko Tabei from Japan became the first woman to reach the summit of Mount Everest.*

🕮 *See 17 May for thoughts on "Abide with me", being a reflection of the gospel passage of Luke 24 (alluded to in today's prayer) - the Risen Jesus walks beside 2 of his followers. At first they don't recognise him.*

🕮 *On this day in 79AD, Mount Vesuvius erupted, burying the Roman city of Pompeii. See a footnote for 1st August.*

🎶 Father, in my life I see *("you walk with me")*; Yahweh, I know you are near *("if I climb to the heavens")*; Walk with me *("shall not fear the steepest mountainside")*

25 AUGUST

1 There is a Buddhist story of a young woman whose baby grew sick and died. She was torn apart with grief and sorrow, and asked a Buddhist holy man if her grief and sorrow would ever go away.

2 *"You must bring me a bowl of rice,"* he said, *"but it must be from a house where no-one has ever suffered the loss of someone they loved and cared for."*

3 So the woman set out, thinking this would be an easy task which would then result, at last, in her grief and sorrow no longer dominating her life. In the first house that she visited she found that a family member had died two years before. They talked, and each felt a little better as they shared their experience and learned from one another and supported each other.

4 In the next house, someone had lost a close friend. Again, she and the family found support. In the third house she began to appreciate more that love costs.

5 And so it went on, from house to house. Eventually the woman returned to the holy man who asked if she had a bowl of rice for him. She had been told to bring one from a house where nobody had ever suffered the loss of someone they loved and cared for. *"No,"* she said. *"Every house I have visited has had people who have suffered the loss of someone they have loved and cared for. What I **have** discovered is that it is because we love greatly that we experience such pain and sorrow when loved ones die. Our pain and sorrow may get less as time goes by, but they never go away. The medicine I have found in visiting other homes is that peace can come from helping others and sharing their problems."*

6 The poet, Alfred Lord Tennyson, wrote:

> *" 'Tis better to have loved and lost*
> *Than never to have loved at all."*

7 *Let us pray:*

Lord Jesus, you tell us
that those who mourn are "blessed",
knowing that only those
who love greatly
can mourn.
We know, too,
that it is better
to have loved and lost someone
than never to have loved at all.
We ask you today
that through our own sufferings
of different kinds,
we may discover
strength and peace
through helping
and supporting others
in their difficulties. Amen.

📖 *The quote is from* "In Memoriam" , *written in 1850 by Alfred Lord Tennyson (1809-1892).*

📖 *2 Cor 1³⁻⁴:* "Blessed be our gentle Father, who is the God of all consolation. He comforts us in all our sorrows, and we can offer that same support and comfort to others who are suffering."

📖 *See also 8 April, and the prayer of 3 August.*

📖 *"Blessed are those who mourn, for they shall be comforted" - Mt 5⁵.*

♩ Be still and know I am with you *("be glad the day you have sorrow")*; I am with you for ever; In you, my God *("my troubles/sorrow will cease")*; O let all who thirst

1 The greatest explosion to occur in modern times took place on the night of 27th/28th August in 1883. The volcano on the island of Krakatoa in Indonesia erupted. It is estimated that the explosion was heard over 8 % of the Earth; certainly it was heard 3,000 miles away (4,800 km). The *"tsunamis"* (often called "tidal waves") reached as high as 35 metres (120 feet), and they travelled 8,000 miles (13,000 km) before dying out. The huge waves killed about 36,000 people.

2 Ash and dust from Krakatoa reached a height of 34 miles (55 km) into the atmosphere. 10 days later, dust fell over 3,000 miles (5,000 km) away. Fine dust was carried around the upper atmosphere for at least 3 years, resulting in brilliant colours in the sunrise and sunset across the world during that time. These coloured skies were caused by the refraction (bending) of the light rays from the sun by the tiny dust particles, in the same way as water droplets in the sky on a sunny day can cause a rainbow.

3 *Let us pray:*

Lord God, Creator of light
at the rising of your sun
each morning,
let the greatest of all lights - your love -
rise, like the sun,
within my heart.
Amen.

A moving personal account of the eruption of and the tragedies associated with the Mount St Helens volcano in the USA (which erupted on 18/5/1980) may be read in the January 1981 'National Geographic' magazine, by Rowe Findley. Well-renowned for its photography, the magazine can also be viewed on the CD-Rom pack of 'The National Geographic - the '80s and '90s'. Part of the article is repeated in the Encarta Deluxe Encyclopaedia.

What are often called "tidal waves" are a misnomer because they are not caused by tides. "Tsunamis" is the correct term.

The eruption of Tambora in 1815 - also in Indonesia - sent 4 times more ash than Krakatoa into the atmosphere, causing "the year without a summer" in 1816.

This is also the day on which the short-lived Albino Luciani was elected Pope John Paul I - 26 August 1978.

 I watch the sunrise

on this day in 1910 was
... up to be Mother Teresa
...o worked with the poor-
... in India.

2 ... once asked Mother Teresa
why she bothered working with the poor
in Calcutta, because it was all just a drop
in the ocean - there being millions of poor
people in India. Mother Teresa said in
reply that she was not concerned with a
big way of doing things - she was concerned with individuals: *"This person"*,
she pointed to someone, *"thinks it makes
all the difference!"*

3 *Let us pray:*

Loving Lord,
   inspire me
   to be welcoming and generous
   in my attitude to others,
   showing individuals
   that they matter and are important.
May I make a difference
   to someone
   in my part of the world today.
Amen.

✍ *Agnes Gonxha Bojaxhiu - Mother Teresa of Calcutta: 27/8/10 - 5/9/97.*

✍ *See also 9 Feb, 4 March, 13 June, 13 July, and 5,12,20 September.*

♪ If I am lacking love; I give my hands

AUGUST 28

1   Today is the feast of St Augustine who was born in 354 AD in the time of the Roman Empire, in what is now the north African country of Algeria.

2   In his lengthy book called *"Confessions"*, Augustine tells us that he was influenced to become a Christian when, somehow, he heard God telling him to *"take up and read"*. Augustine started to read the Bible and discovered God. The example and prayers of his mother Monica (whose feastday it was yesterday) contributed to his becoming a Christian at the age of 33.

3   Augustine wrote these words:

> *"Leave the past to God's mercy,*
> *the present to his love,*
> *and the future to his providence."*

4   *Let us pray:*

Lord, we give you thanks
for the assurance
that the past
can be left to your mercy,
the present to your love,
and the future to your providence.
Help us to grow more aware
of your loving presence,
that we may live more authentically
and proclaim
by our words and actions
the good news
of the fullness of your love.
We ask this through Christ our Lord.
Amen.

✍ *It is thought that Augustine was born 13/11/ 354, and died 28/8/430. It was in the year 395 that Augustine, aged 41, was made Bishop of Hippo (nowadays being the town of Annaba in Algeria). St Augustine of Hippo should not, of course, be confused with St Augustine of Canterbury.*

✍ *"Leave the past..." are words that can easily be learned by heart and often made into a prayer. Augustine also said:*
    "Hate the sin
    but love the sinner."

✍ *On this day in 1963, Martin Luther King gave his "I have a dream..." speech - see 4 April.*

🎵 For to those who love God (*"not the past, the present, nor the future"*); The love I have for you

153

29 AUGUST

1 On this day in 1931, Gandhi, the great Indian leader, visited London. He had called off the campaign of civil disobedience under British rule in India, in order to attend this meeting about the future of his country which was then governed by Britain. A prayerful man, Gandhi wrote these words about prayer:

2 *I am neither a man of letters,*
nor of Science,
but I humbly claim to be a man of prayer.
It is prayer that has saved my life.
Without prayer
I would have lost my reason
a long time ago.
I did not lose my peace of soul
- in spite of many trials -
because the peace
came to me from prayer.

3 *One can live several days without food,*
but not without prayer.
Prayer is the key to each morning,
and the lock to every evening.
This is my teaching:
let everyone try this experience
and they will find that daily prayer
will add something new to their lives.

4 *Let us pray:*

Lord Jesus,
  your friends said to you:
  "Teach us how to pray".
We ask that you give us
  the fullness of your Spirit
  to help us to pray,
  so that we may grow
  in friendship with you.
Amen.

📖 *For Gandhi, see also 29,30 January (which together give a biography); 5,17 February; 12 May; 28 July.*

📖 *"A man of letters" refers to someone bearing letters after their name, generally signifying having a degree or special award. Gandhi was saying that he was a simple, ordinary person.*

📖 *Gandhi never looked in a mirror. He had it in mind that he could know of himself through what he found reflected in others.*

📖 *India (and Pakistan) achieved independence on 15 August 1947.*

🎼 Do not worry *("trust and pray")*; In you, my God; Lord, Jesus Christ, you have come to us *("teach us how to pray")*; Sing a simple song

1 It is reckoned that about 300 million people throughout the world drink Coca-Cola every day. It was invented by Doctor John Pemberton of Atlanta, Georgia, in the USA. He had set out to create a medicine that cured hangovers!

2 Pemberton knew that people living high up in the mountains of Peru and Bolivia chewed the dried leaves of the COCA bush, mixing them with a little lime or wood ash. That mixture acted as a stimulant, especially in the low-oxygen atmosphere of the Andes mountains. Pemberton started his drinks mixture with these coca leaves.

3 The COLA tree is found in tropical countries, and produces seeds (called nuts) that are about 2.5cm (1 inch) long. The brown seeds smell like nutmeg but are bitter, and contain tannin (also found in tea) and caffeine (found in both tea and coffee). Cola nuts are also chewed as a stimulant.

4 Pemberton mixed together extracts from the coca leaves and the cola nuts, adding some secret ingredients of oils and juices which, together, made a syrup. He named the concentrated syrup *"Coca-Cola"*, and people added soda (or fizzy water) to it. He patented the name, but only 112 litres of the drink were sold in its first year. Pemberton sold most of his Coca-Cola shares because he needed the money at that time. Shortly afterwards a businessman called Asa Candler bought up all the shares, knowing that what was needed was advertising. The drink began to become popular.

5 In 1899 two baseball fans, Benjamin Thomas and Joseph Whitehead, realised that huge quantities of Coca-Cola could be bought and consumed at sports stadiums. They bought the exclusive rights to bottle and sell the drink, and then Coca-Cola spread throughout the United States. Thomas and Whitehead and es-pecially Candler became very rich. Candler had paid 1,000 dollars for all the Coca-Cola shares. 25 years later, in 1912, he sold them for 25 million dollars.

6 Coca-Cola was soon produced in many countries. Tomorrow, 31st August, marks the anniversary in 1900 of Coca Cola being introduced into Britain.

7 The secret of the success of Coca-Cola and most other products has been the advertising, but, of course, we do need to be selective and not be taken in by everything that is designed to catch our eyes.

8 *Let us pray:*

Lord Jesus,
 in the world that you love so much
 we are surrounded with advertising
 on the streets, in magazines,
 on TV and on the Internet
 - all trying to convince us
 of ways of enjoying ourselves
 and becoming likeable and popular.

9 **Keep our vision clear**
 and show us how to distinguish
 between what is shallow
 and what is of lasting value.
Inspire us
 to choose ways of deeper happiness
 that lead to fullness of life.
We ask this of you who said:
 "I am the way, the truth and the life".
Amen.

❖❖❖❖❖❖❖❖❖❖❖❖❖❖❖❖❖❖❖

📖 *The tropical cola tree is related to that which produces cocoa, from which we make chocolate.*

📖 "The world that you love so much" - "God so loved the world that he sent his Son..." *(John 3[16])*

🎵 My Lord, my Master *("food for the journey")*; Seek ye first

1 In the early hours of Sunday 31st August 1997, news came through of the tragic death in a car accident of Diana, Princess of Wales, aged 36.

2 Cardinal Basil Hume spoke the following words later, and we can remember our own loved ones:

"Faith admits us into death's secrets.
Death is not the end of the road,
but a gateway to a better place.
It is in this place
that our noblest aspirations
will be realised.
It is here that we will understand
how our experiences
of goodness, love, beauty and joy
are realities which exist perfectly in God.
It is in heaven
that we shall rest in him,
and our hearts will be restless
until they rest in God.
We, left to continue
our pilgrimage through life,
weep and mourn.
You, Diana, and your companions, too,
are on your way to union with him
who loves you so.
He knows the love
which you, Diana, had for others.
God speaks now of his love for you.
Our tears
will not be bitter ones now,
but a gentle weeping
to rob our sadness of its agony
and lead at last to peace,
peace with God."

3 Princess Diana had said:

"There are two important things in life:
kindness in another's trouble,
and courage in your own."

4 *Let us pray:*

Lord, I ask
for the power of your Spirit in my life
that I may live in such a way
that I show kindness
in another's trouble,
and courage in my own.
Amen.

✍ *Cardinal Hume's words are from a meditation that was broadcast after the Princess' death. "Our hearts will be restless until they rest in God" is a reference to St Augustine's prayer. "You awaken us to delight in your praises, for you have made us for yourself, and our hearts are restless until they rest in you."*

✍ *See 6 September, being the date in 1997 on which the funeral of the Princess was held in Westminster Abbey.*

✍ *Princess Diana told Dame Thora Hird that her favourite hymn was "Breathe on me, breath of God".*

✍ *Poem: Rupert Brooke - 'The Soldier': "If I should die, think only this of me..."*

♩ Abide with me; Be still and know I am with you; Breathe on me, breath of God; Breath of God, O Holy Spirit; In you, my God

Moveable
Feasts

ASCENSION

1 For 40 days after Jesus had risen from the dead, he was seen by many people. Today's feast recalls his return to God the Father. We read in the New Testament that Jesus now *"sits at the right hand of God the Father"* and there prays for us.

2 *Let us pray:*

God our Father, to those who love you
  everything works out for good,
  because you have chosen us
  to bear the image of Jesus, your Son,
  who not only died for us
  but rose from the dead,
  and now sits at your right hand,
  praying for us,
  as we recall
  on this Ascension Day.

3 And so, with you on our side,
  who can be against us?
Even if we face hard times
  or are threatened
  - your love is greater still,
  and nothing can ever separate us
  from your love.
Even in difficulties, Father,
  we can never be failures or losers
  because of the power of your love.

4 As the Feast of Pentecost approaches,
  we ask you, Father,
  to fill us to overflowing
  with your Holy Spirit,
  that we may be empowered
  to be the people you call us to be,
  and enabled to fulfil
  the calling and mission
  that you have for each one of us.
Amen.

📖 *The first two paragraphs of the prayer are based on Romans 8[28-39] by St Paul.*

📖 *When we read of "God" in the New Testament we understand "God the Father". In the New Testament we find a number of references to Jesus "at the right hand of God" (the Father) after the period that followed his Resurrection: Mk 6[19], Lk 22[69], Acts 7[55,56], Rom 8[34], Col 3[1], Heb 1[3], Heb 10[12], 1 Pet 3[22].*

📖 "If I could hear Christ praying for me in the next room, I would not fear a million enemies. Yet distance makes no difference he is praying for me."

R.M.McCheyne

📖 *Ascension is celebrated in many countries on the Thursday which is the 40th day after Easter, as we read that the Ascension took place 40 days after the Resurrection - see Acts 1[3,9-11]. Some countries transfer the celebration to the nearest Sunday.*

📖 *The following words are based on a reflection thought to be by G.K.Chesterton:*

'When Jesus returned to his Father,
perhaps his Father said to him:
"Son, what was the worst of it all?
Was it the nails?"
"No, Father,
the hardest thing wasn't the nails,
it was the kiss of betrayal
- the kiss from someone I had trusted
as a close friend." '

📖 *William Temple, former Archbishop of Canterbury (1942-44), wrote:*
"The Ascension of Christ is his liberation from all restrictions of time and space. It does not represent his removal from earth, but his constant presence everywhere on earth."

🎵 Follow me *("although I go away")*; For to those who love God; If God is for us

PENTECOST

1 Pentecost is sometimes known as the *'Birthday of the Church'* because this day celebrates when God's people were empowered in a special way by the Spirit to carry on from where Jesus left off. As in a relay race, the "baton" is passed on from Jesus himself to his followers. They are now alive with the Spirit, enabled to do what they would not have been able to do simply by themselves. We cannot live as God would have us live, just by our own efforts and gifts and determination. We need the life and power of the Spirit.

2 Three symbols are sometimes used to represent the Holy Spirit.

3 **FIRE** is like the Spirit - spreading quickly, giving light and warmth, flickering as though invisible, fusing together what otherwise would remain separate.

4 A **DOVE** is like the Spirit - gentle, graceful, free to go wherever it wishes.

5 **WIND or BREATH** is like the Spirit - necessary for us to live; direct contact (like mouth-to-mouth rescusitation) brings life to people. The wind is like the Spirit because it is strong and invisible. As with windmills, the Spirit brings power, enabling us to do what we could not do simply by ourselves.

6 *Let us pray:*

God our Father,
this feastday celebrates
the pouring out of the Holy Spirit
on the first community
of those who really believed
that Jesus was risen from the dead
and who could say
that "Jesus is Lord".

7 On this day
your Spirit empowered the apostles
to be fully alive,

and the Spirit's gift of courage
overpowered their fear of others
and their anxiety about the future.

8 They received gifts
of knowledge,
wisdom and understanding,
and the ability
to make balanced judgments
- all enabling them
to convey well to others
the Good News
of your overwhelming love
and acceptance and forgiveness.

9 May your Spirit lead us
to have great respect and reverence
for all creation, for each person,
and for you, our God.

10 Open our eyes in wonder and awe
at all that is around us,
so that all that we see
may lead us to grow in awareness
of your loving presence with us.

11 And so
we ask you today, generous Father,
to fill us to overflowing
with your Spirit,
that we may be empowered
to be the people you call us to be,
and enabled to fulfil
the calling and mission
that you have for each one of us.

12 Rooted in Jesus
and making good use of the gifts
of the Holy Spirit,
may we then
bear many good fruits,
such as love and joy,
peace and patience,
kindness and faithfulness,
gentleness, goodness,
and self-control. Amen.

- *An alternative prayer can be found on 18th January, or:*

13 **Come, Holy Spirit, fill our hearts
and set us alight
with the fire of your love
that, in our own way,
we may renew
our own part of the world. Amen.**

- *Or, with a group joining in the response:*

14 **Amongst our run-down neighbourhoods
and our polluted earth:
*Spirit of God,
renew the face of the earth.***

15 **Amongst our politicians and leaders:
*Spirit of God,
renew the face of the earth.***

16 **Amongst people
for whom hatred and violence
dominate their lives.
*Spirit of God,
renew the face of the earth.***

17 **Amongst those who are ill
or worn out.
Amongst those who are lonely
or depressed,
anxious or without hope.
*Spirit of God,
renew the face of the earth.***

18 **In our workplaces,
and amongst those
who are unemployed:
*Spirit of God,
renew the face of the earth.***

19 **In our creativity
and in our recreation;
in our prayer and in our relationships:
*Spirit of God,
renew the face of the earth.***

20 **In our homes
and amongst our families and friends:
*Spirit of God,
renew the face of the earth.***

📖 *See 8th June for the Jewish Feast of Pentecost. It was on the Jewish Feast of Pentecost that the apostles were gathered in the Upper Room, and there received the Spirit. Christians retained the name of the feast, and the Christian Pentecost now occurs 10 days after Ascension Thursday. At Pentecost the colour of vestments for the Eucharist is red, being a sign of the warmth of the fire of the Spirit.*

📖 *For centuries, Easter and Pentecost were the main days on which adults received the Sacrament of Baptism. In those times Baptism was by total immersion in water and, in England's cold climate, understandably it became preferable to have this form of Baptism not at Easter, but 50 days later at Pentecost, when it would be a little warmer. As the adults to be baptised wore white robes on that day alone, Pentecost in England was associated with the colour white, and became known as "Whit-Sunday", from the Anglo-Saxon "hwita Sunnandaeg".*

📖 *Some processions of Christian witness and solidarity are still held at Pentecost. On that day a procession takes place along Hope Street between Liverpool's Catholic and Anglican Cathedrals, starting in one cathedral and finishing in the other (reversing the order the following year).*

📖 *"Spirit of God, renew the face of the earth" - see Psalm 103/104[30]. 7 gifts of the Spirit are listed in Isaiah 11[1-3]. 12 fruits of the Spirit are listed in Galatians 5[22]. Could look through newspapers and magazines to link articles with particular fruits of the Spirit.*

📖 *Poem - "God's grandeur" by G.M.Hopkins*

🎼 Breath of God, O Holy Spirit; Come down O love divine; Follow me; God's Spirit is in my heart; O let all who thirst; O living water; Spirit of the living Christ; This is what Yahweh asks of you

TRINITY SUNDAY

1 On this day we call to mind that the one
God is Father, Son and Holy Spirit - three
Persons in One God. St Ignatius of Loyola
said that *"as three musical notes played
together produce only one sound; likewise,
there are three Persons in one God."*

2 *Let us pray to the Father, Son and
Spirit, Three Persons in One God:*

3 God the Father,
  you welcome us by name   Is 43¹
  and care for us individually.
You are the Father of Jesus
  and you are our Father, too,
  saying to us as you did to your Son
  that we are your well-loved
  sons and daughters.   Lk 3²²
You invite us to the very best
  that the relationship of father
  can offer.

4 Jesus, God the Son,
  you give us light in our darkness Jn 8¹²
  and hope in our difficulties,
  because even the power of death
  could not hold
  or defeat you.
One of our greatest needs
  is to be free,
  and so we ask you today
  to show us
  the freedom that you bring,   Jn8³⁶
  and the life
  that you invite us to have
  to the full.   Jn 10¹⁰
You promise to be with us always   Mt 28²⁰
  and guide and protect us
  as a shepherd.   Jn 10⁷·¹¹
You are our Brother
  and you invite us to the very best
  that the relationshp of brother
  can offer.

5 God the Holy Spirit,
  it is not by any strength of our own
  but by the free gift
  of your life and power
  and your strength and courage,
  that we are enabled to do
  what we are called to do.
We could not live
  as we are invited to live
  simply by
  our own efforts
  and gifts and determination.
Jesus tells us
  that you are within us,
  and so we pray
  that whatever
  contradicts your presence
  may be changed,
  so that you
  may be fully present within.

6 For the creating of the Father (+)
  and the healing of the Son
  and the empowering of the Holy Spirit,
  we give thanks.
Amen.

An alternative prayer:

7   I make the Sign of the Cross,
    placing myself in the presence
    of the One God,
    Father, Son and Holy Spirit,
    renewing my commitment
    to do all things
    in the name (+) of the Father above
    and of the Son beside
    and of the Holy Spirit within.
    Amen.

*Or a greeting/blessing that is often called
"the Grace" and is found in 2 Cor 13^{13}:*

8   The grace of the Lord Jesus Christ,
    the love of God,
    and the fellowship of the Holy Spirit
    be with us all.   Amen.

Or could adapt Prayer 15 from the Appendix of 70 Prayers in this volume.

*Another alternative is the following Kikuyu
prayer. The Kikuyu are the largest indigenous group of people in Kenya. They are
mentioned by name in the film, "Out of
Africa" about the Danish Baroness Karen
Blixen and her successes and failures on a
coffee plantation in what is now Kenya:*

9   O Father, your power is greater
        than all powers.
    O Son, under your leadership
        we cannot fear anything.
    O Spirit, under your protection
        there is nothing
        we cannot overcome. Amen.

📖 *Mention in the New Testament of Father, Son
and Spirit together can be found in: Mt 3^{16}, Acts
7^{55}, 2 Cor 13^{13}.*

📖 *"The Spirit dwells within you" - Jn 14^{17}.
"Where the Spirit of the Lord is, there is
freedom" - 2 Cor 3^{17}.
"Unbind him; let him go free" - Jn 11^{44};
see also Lk 4^{18}, Jn 8^{36}, Rom 8^{21}, Eph 1^{7}.*

📖 *John Wesley (17/6/1703 - 2/3/1791), the founder
of the Methodist Church, wrote; "Tell me how
it is that in this room there are three candles
and but one light, and I will explain to you
the mode of the divine existence."*

📖 *Trinity Sunday is the Sunday after Pentecost.*

🎼 Father, in my life I see; God's Spirit is in
my heart; If God is for us; Take my hands
("serve the Trinity above"); This day God
gives me *("threeness of persons")*; This,
then, is my prayer; Praise to the Father

THE BODY & BLOOD OF CHRIST

1   Today is the Feast of the Body and Blood
    of Christ. We recall that Jesus' command
    was to *"take and eat and drink; do this in
    memory of me."*

2   It is because of that command
    that people have found
    no better thing to do
    than to celebrate the Eucharist, the Mass
    - for someone who has died;
    - for the success of an operation;
    - on a couple's wedding day;
    - for a sick person about to die.

3   Down the ages
    people have found no better thing to do
    than celebrate the Eucharist
    - before they were led to the lions
    in the arenas of the Roman Empire;
    - and in hiding
    during Reformation times
    400 years ago
    as they faced imprisonment or death;
    - and on the beaches at Dunkirk in 1940
    as men were bombed and shot
    around them;
    - and in secrecy in the death-camps
    of Hitler and Stalin;
    - and in the darkness of night
    by a bishop in China,
    tortured and imprisoned for his faith.

4   And we could find today
    in a congregation at Mass
    - people who are giving thanks
    for a successful outcome
    to what they are worried about;
    - individuals in pain and anger
    at the suffering
    others have brought to them;
    - people who have many questions
    and are searching for meaning
    in their lives;
    - individuals who trust,
    even though life is difficult for them;
    - people who are asking for forgiveness,

or who feel the need around them
of others who are searching.

5   All these
    have been carrying out Jesus' command
    to *"take and eat and drink in memory of
    me."*
    Let's pause for a moment...

✍ *This reflection is inspired by words of Dom
Gregory Dix in 'The Shape of the Liturgy', A &
C Black, 1945.*

✍ *This feast is still sometimes called "Corpus
Christi" from the Latin for "the Body of Christ".
It is usually celebrated on the Thursday after
Trinity Sunday, although some countries trans-
fer the feast to the following Sunday.*

✍ *Jesus' command was to "take and eat" but an
over-emphasis on our unworthiness (rather
than focussing on God's mercy and loving kindness) in the five centuries prior to Vatican II in
the 1960s gave rise to Communion rarely being received at Mass. To display belief in Jesus' Real Presence, Corpus Christi processions
were held. The Blessed Sacrament was dis-
played in a monstrance (a Latin word meaning
"to show") for the people to venerate. Since
Vatican II and the return to the sources of the
liturgy, the majority of people do now receive
Holy Communion (the Body and Blood of Christ)
at the Eucharist. Jesus' command to "take and
eat" now receives greater emphasis than wish-
ing only to **look** at the Blessed Sacrament and
receive a blessing although, of course, one does
not exclude the other.*

✍ *See also Holy Thursday (Vol. 1) and 21 July.*

🎵 Because the Lord is my shepherd *(ban-
quet)*; I am the bread of life; In bread
we bring you, Lord; Godhead here in
hiding; Lord Jesus Christ, you have come
to us *("you have commanded us to do")*;
This is my body

THE SACRED HEART OF JESUS

1 On this feastday each year, some Catholics in the mountainous Tyrol region of western Austria, light fires high up in the mountains. The fires can be seen for miles around. They are lit as a sign of the warmth of the love of Jesus. As the "heart" is a symbol of love on Valentine's Day, this feast of "the Sacred Heart of Jesus" focuses on his love and acceptance and forgiveness.

2 *Let us pray:*

Lord Jesus,
when I become particularly conscious
of my difficulties
and limitations and worries,
when life seems to crowd in on me
and I become more conscious
of my failures,
convince me in my heart
that *"love never fails"*   *1 Cor 13[8]*
- that there is "success"
whenever I love generously.

3 Lead me to grow in the faith deep-down
that you love me today - as I am -
in the reality of my life this day,
and then,
living in your perfect love,
any fears and anxieties
will be cast away,   *1 Jn 4[18]*
and I will bear your fruit
in plenty. Amen   *Jn 18[5,9]*

📖 *Peter van Breemen's book, 'As Bread that is Broken' (Dimension Books, 1978, page 9), talks of our uniqueness and acceptance by God, slow as we are to really take that in, e.g. "I am accepted by God as I am - **as I am** - and not as I should be... He loves me with my ideals and disappointments, my sacrifices and my joys, my successes and my failures..."* adding that it is one thing for us to "know" that we are accepted, but quite another thing to grow in the "faith" that that it is so. Essentially, of course, God does not need us to be "worthy" (as if we could be!) for him to love us 100%.

📖 *"There is no surprise more magical than the surprise of being loved; it is God's finger on a person's shoulder." - Charles Morgan.*

📖 *"There is no pit so deep*
that Christ's love is not deeper still"
- Corrie Ten Boom, Dutch spiritual writer and former concentration-camp victim of the Nazis. Her books include "The Hiding Place" (also made into an inspiring film).

📖 *The word "love" appears in 297 verses in the Old Testament, and 168 verses of the New Testament: a total of 428 times (JB). Many scripture passages focus on the love of Jesus, including:*
- Lk 19[1-10] - Zacchaeus - see 23 Feb.
- 1 Cor 12[31]-14[1] - Love is...
- Romans 8 - see 29 June.
- Ephesians 3[14-21] - to grasp the breadth, length, height and depth of God's love.
- 1 John 4[7-19] - God loved us first; our love is a response to his.
May we never live in such a way that anyone could ever say of us: "You have no love of God in you" (Jn 5[42]).

📖 *Since about 1700 it became popular to devote the First Friday of each month to the Sacred Heart of Jesus. In days when frequent Communion was rare, some people sought to receive Communion on nine consecutive first Fridays. This practice is reflected in many parishes as special visits are made to the sick and housebound on the first Friday of each month, taking Communion (the Body of Christ) to those people.*

📖 *This feast is celebrated on the Friday following the Second Sunday after Pentecost.*

🎼 If I am lacking love; In you, my God *("the fire of your love")*; Oh the love of my Lord; Shine, Jesus, shine; The light of Christ; The love I have for you *(Only a shadow)*;

PRAYERS FOR USE BY TEACHERS & OTHERS

- *for personal prayer, for times when staff pray together, for inclusion on staff or parental briefings/newsletters…, for certain occasions e.g. sickness, death, Leavers' Presentation…*

CALLING TO MIND GOD'S PRESENCE

1 - *GP*

TWO OR THREE GATHERED

Lord Jesus, you promised
  that when two or three
  would get together in your name
  then you would be present with them.
May your Spirit
  lead us to grow more aware
  of your presence in our lives
  today and every day. Amen.

2 - *GP*

THE PRESENCE OF GOD

Let us remember
that we are in the presence of God.
And let us adore him.

3 - *GP*

IN GOD'S PRESENCE

Lord Jesus,
  help me to grow more aware
  of your life-giving presence,
  so that my attitude
  and words and actions
  may better reflect yours.
Enable me to live in such a way today
  that, however dimly,
  others may see you in me. Amen.

*see also Prayers 27 & 39, and the reflections
and prayers of 10 Feb; 8,17,27,31 March; 24
May; 4,24,28 Aug.*

4 - O

THE GRAIL PRAYER

Lord Jesus,
I give you my hands - to do your work.
I give you my feet - to go your way.
I give you my eyes - to see as you do.
I give you my tongue - to speak your words.
I give you my mind
   - that you may think in me.
I give you my spirit
   - that you may pray in me.
Above all, I give you my heart
   that you may love, in me,
   your Father and all mankind.
I give you my whole self
   that you may grow in me,
   so that it is you, Lord Jesus,
   who live and work and pray in me. Amen.

5 - O

A MORNING OFFERING

God our Father, open our eyes
   to the splendour of your creation,
   to the dignity of those
   who are made
   in your image and likeness,
   and to the opportunities each day brings.
Create new miracles this day
   that, transformed by your Spirit
   living within us,
   we may touch the hearts
   of those you have entrusted to us.
Help us all
   to walk more faithfully in your presence
   and seek first your kingdom,
   with Jesus your Son. Amen.

6 - O

PRAYER OF A TEACHER BEFORE SCHOOL

Lord, you are my patience, my strength,
   my light and my counsel.
You guide me in what I have to say
   to my students,
and you make them responsive
   to my words.

Be with them and with me
   at all times.
Give me - for their sake -
   a share in the gifts of your Holy Spirit:
   of wisdom, understanding,
   counsel, courage,
   knowledge,
   filial devotion to you,
   and a desire not to displease you.
Increase my faith
   and give me enthusiasm
   to build your kingdom. Amen.

7 - O

"SUCCESS" AND "FAILURE"

Father,
   into your hands we place our successes.
Into your hands we also place our failures,
   and we pray that, through your Spirit,
   we may face the challenges of life
   with courage and determination.
Help us to think anew
   and see things more broadly
   than in terms of "success"
   and "failure",
   and focus more on "faithfulness".
Lead us always to trust
   and place ourselves confidently
   in your hands. Amen.

8 - O

WISDOM, TALENTS, SERVICE, PRIORITIES

Lord, you have enriched our lives
   in many ways.
Give us this day
   the wisdom to recognise
   which things are important
   and which things are not.
Show us how best
   to use the time and talents
   you have given us.
Help us to use all opportunities wisely
   that we may give in service to others
   the good gifts
   we have received from you. Amen.

FOR OUR STUDENTS

9 - S
THAT OUR YOUNG PEOPLE MAY GROW

Father,
> preserve in our young people
> a sense of wonder at the marvels of life.

Bless them,
> that they may grow in your love
> and in concern and service
> for the good of others.

Teach them to discern good from evil
> that they may grow
> in integrity of character,
> and develop a true sense of values
> through following Jesus,
> your Son and our Brother.   Amen.

10 - S
TO HAVE VISION AND BE DISCERNING

God our Father, our young people
> are surrounded with advertising
> in magazines, on the streets,
> on TV and on the Internet,
> all trying to convince them
> of ways of enjoying themselves,
> of being more likeable
> and achieving lasting happiness
> and fulfilment.

We ask you to help our young people
> to see clearly and be discerning,
> making wise choices
> and balanced judgements. Amen.

11 - S
GROWING IN FAITH, CONFIDENCE AND RESPECT OF OTHERS

God our Father,
> enable our young people
> to live the vision
> that you have for each of them,
> and lead them to grow in confidence
> in who they are,
> and in the faith
> that you call each of them by name.

Show them how to live in such a way
> that they respect and accept others
> for who they are.

Inspire them
> to be generous in praising other people
> and in showing appreciation
> for the efforts and achievements
> of others.   Amen.

12 - S
SELF-ESTEEM AND SELF-CONFIDENCE

God our Father,
> may the care we express as teachers
> confirm for the young people
> their own value,
> so that they may be helped
> to feel good about themselves
> and grow
> in self-esteem and self-confidence
> and experience success.

Inspire them to use well
> their education
> and all the challenges and opportunities
> that come to them.

Lead them to grow in thankfulness
> for all that they are,
> for all that they receive,
> and for the people
> who are a positive influence
> in their lives.   Amen.

13
DIFFICULTIES IN RELATING

Lord,
> I can't seem to get anywhere with *Jenny*
> - nor *she* with me.

I must admit
> that I don't find much
> that is likeable in *her*,
> and I'm sure that *she* doesn't see
> anything likeable in me.

I need the gifts of your Spirit
> to help me to look on *her*
> as you look on *her*,
> to be patient,

to show the better side of my nature,
and to be able to trust
that, whilst nothing good
might seem to come at present,
something may bear fruit
in months or years to come.
I need your Spirit
that I may never say or do anything
which I would regret later.
May more of *your* attitude
shine through me this day. Amen.

14 - S
A STUDENT IN DIFFICULTY

Loving Father,
we read that you treasure
and hold a special place
for each and every person,
as though only that one individual exists.
And so I thank you for _____
who is very close to you,
even though *she* may not realise it.
Help *her* to overcome the difficulties
she finds in school.
Break down the barriers
that are keeping *her*
from making good progress.
Clear *her* mind
so that *she* can concentrate
and work to the best of *her* ability.
Give me wisdom,
patience and understanding,
so that I may lead *her* forward.
Inspire me
to promote the best in *her*
and give praise and encouragement,
that *she* may feel confident
in my care and concern. Amen.

15 - S
PRAYING SPONTANEOUSLY WITH
AN INDIVIDUAL

*(example, praying to the Father, the Son and the
Holy Spirit:)*

Father, you have made *Michael*
in your own image and likeness,
and when you look at *him*
you look on *him* with great love.
From all time
you have had *him* in mind
and you call *him* by *his* name.
At Jesus' baptism in the River Jordan
you were heard to say:
"This is my well-loved Son."
And I thank you, Father,
that, today,
you speak in the same way
to *Michael* as well:
that *he* is your *son*
whom you love so much...

Lord Jesus, you said
that when two or three
get together in your name
then you would be with them,
and I thank you, Lord,
that you are with us both now...
When you walked around Galilee
you saw people
who were ill or in difficulty,
and you brought
peace and healing to them.
I ask you today
to stretch out your hand
and touch *Michael*
in the way that you know is best...

Holy Spirit,
you give help and strength
that enables people
to make good progress.
I ask today
that you live fully in _____,
enabling *him* to live
as the person you are calling *him* to be.
Bless *him* with your gifts
of wisdom, knowledge
and understanding,
that he may come to appreciate
himself and others more fully...

16 - S
BLESSINGS OF KNOWLEDGE, WISDOM AND COMPASSION

Lord,
we ask for your blessing
on all the young people
entrusted to our care.
We ask you to give them
the gifts of knowledge and wisdom
and understanding.
What we pray for,
may they be determined to work at,
so that they develop
an open mind,
a thirst for knowledge,
and a wisdom that makes good use
of their knowledge and experience.
We know that any gifts are useless
without compassion
and concern for others,
and so we ask you
to inspire our young people
to live a life for others
that is worthwhile
Amen.

17 - S
A BLESSING FOR STUDENTS

May the Lord bless you in the years ahead
and inspire you
to be positive in your attitude,
faithful in loving
and generous in the service of others.
May you learn from the difficulties
that you will face,
and so grow
in wisdom and understanding
and in compassion for others.
May you be patient
and forgiving in your relationships.
May you live in such a way
that the words "thanks" and "sorry"
come readily to you.

May you retain
a sense of wonder and awe,
and may you grow as the person
God calls you to be. Amen.

18 - S
A TEACHER'S NIGHT PRAYER

Lord,
I pray for your blessing
on all the young people
you have entrusted to my care.
As they sleep, Lord,
may they be refreshed for tomorrow,
healed of hurts,
soothed from fears,
and secure in the wealth of your love.
Amen.

FOR STUDENTS & TEACHERS

19 - *ST*

LOVING OURSELVES AND OTHERS

Father,
enable us to see and love
ourselves and others
as you see and love us,
and so may we grow
in the image and likeness
of Jesus your Son and our Brother. Amen.

20 - *ST*

LEARNING ALONGSIDE THE YOUNG

Lord, inspire us
    to learn alongside the young people
    you have entrusted to our care.
May all that we learn together today
    draw us closer to one another
    and to you. Amen.

21 - *ST*

FOR OUR SCHOOL COMMUNITY

Father,
    we thank you for our school community,
    knowing that
    we can learn from each other
    and grow in faith.
We pray for all involved in our school,
    that all of us may grow
    as the people you call us to be.
Amen.

22 - *ST*

GROWING TOGETHER IN JESUS

Father,
    we ask for your blessing
    on all who are involved in our school.
May your Spirit inspire us
    to follow your Way together,
    discover your Truth together,
    and grow together
    in the fullness of Life
    offered by Jesus your Son.
Amen.

23 - *ST*

THE TREASURES WE HAVE BEEN GIVEN; BRINGING OUT THE BEST IN ONE ANOTHER

God our Father, in saying
    that you have written our names
    on the palm of your hands,
    you are telling us that each person
    is unique and special to you.
We pray for students and staff
    that we may all discover in ourselves
    the treasures you have given us,
    and develop and put to good use
    the qualities we hold in trust from you.
We pray
    and commit ourselves today, Father,
    to promote goodness and happiness,
    by treating others
    with respect
    and care and understanding.
So may we help
    to bring out the best in one another.
Amen.

24 - *ST*

TREATING WITH RESPECT, CARE AND UNDERSTANDING

Lord Jesus, we ask for
    the life and power of your Spirit
    in our school,
    so that adults and young people alike
    may always see the need
    to treat others generously,
    with respect and courtesy
    and care and understanding.
As you cured people who were blind,
    lead us to focus on the positive
    rather than the negative,
    so that we may all
    bring out the best in one another.
Amen.

25 - *ST*
PROMOTING ALL THAT IS LIFE-GIVING

Lord Jesus,
give us the power and life of your Spirit
that we may live more fully
and may more readily
promote all that is life-giving
in the young people
who are entrusted to our care.
Amen.

26 - *ST*
COMPARING SELF NOT WITH OTHERS
BUT WITH MY OWN POTENTIAL

Lord, may each of our students
respond well to your invitation
to live fully
and make the best use
of their skills and talents.
Show them that rather than
draw comparisons with others,
each person
is called to look at their own potential.
Inspire all of us to be generous
in praising others
for the good use of their abilities
- looking not so much
at the degree of achievement
but at the effort put in.
Amen.

FOR OURSELVES AS TEACHERS

27 - T
CALLED TO HOLINESS

Lord, you call us by name,
and you call us to holiness
as you did *(e.g. patron saint of school)*.
We ask you to fill us with your Spirit
so that we, too,
may reflect the life of your Son
in our thoughts and attitude
and in our words and actions.
Lead us to grow more aware
of your presence in our lives,
and empower us to bring
the good news of your love and salvation
to all those you have entrusted to us.
Amen.

28 - T
FOR DISCERNMENT

Grant us, O Lord,
to know what is worth knowing,
to love what is worth loving,
to praise what delights you most,
to value what is precious in your sight,
and to hate what is offensive to you.
Do not let us judge by what we see,
nor pass sentence
according to what we hear,
but to judge rightly
between things that differ. Amen.
(Thomas à Kempis: 1380-1471)

29 - T
LOVING WORDS

Lord,
may the words we use
today and every day
be words of kindness,
words of humour and goodwill:
words that come from the overflowing
of a loving heart. Amen.

30 - T
ENCOURAGING OTHERS

Lord, we ask you to inspire us
to encourage others today
in our attitude and words and actions.
Amen.

31 - T
HOW I MIGHT LIVE

Lord, give me patience and tolerance
with everyone.
Lead me to be kind and generous
to everyone,
and keep me cheerful
for the sake of everyone. Amen.

32 - T
TO LOVE AND CARE

God our Father,
help us to appreciate
that those you have entrusted to us
are your sons and daughters.
Inspire us to take even more care
over their education
than if they were the children of a king.
Help us to show,
by the care we take of them,
that we have a real love for them,
a great tenderness towards them.
May we show much kindness,
and may love guide us in all our actions.
Inspire us
to build on the affection
that the young people have for us
to guide them to you. Amen.
*(Phrased from words of John Baptist
De La Salle, the patron saint of teachers)*

33 - T
TOUCHING HEARTS

Father, teach us
    to help young people
    to appreciate their own worth.
Enable us to touch their hearts
    and empower us
    to reveal your love for them.
Inspire us to support and encourage
    and build others up.
Help us to follow Christ our Teacher,
    and be credible witnesses of your love.
Amen.

34 - T
REMEMBERED FOR OUR ATTITUDE

Lord,
    most of us
    will not become well-known
    or be written about
    because of great achievements,
    but we will be remembered
    for our attitude towards individuals.
Inspire us, Lord, to live in your presence
    so that we may transform this day
    by being positive in attitude,
    looking for the best
    in people and situations. Amen.

35 - T
JESUS, MY TEACHER

Jesus, my Teacher,
    I come to you today to learn;
    teach me how to follow you, Lord.
When I speak too much,
    teach me to listen to your words.
When I worry about
    the things in my life,
    teach me always to trust in you.
When I cannot sense
    that you are present with me,
    teach me never to give up hope.
Jesus, Bread of Life,
    my Shepherd and Friend,

pick me up when I fall down;
    reach out to me when I am sinking;
    hold me when I am lost.
Jesus, be part of my dreams for the future:
    be a part of my life-story;
    be a part of the story of our school.
In our friendship - Jesus, be with us.
In our failures - Jesus, be with us.
In our successes - Jesus, be with us.
At all moments - walk beside us.
Teach us your ways, Lord.
Teach us to be faithful.
Teach us
    to treasure our friendship with you.
Amen.

(G.Gamble)

36 - T
"LET THE CHILDREN COME TO ME"?

Were you joking, Lord,
    when you set a child in front of adults
    and told them to become as children?
Some of the young people
    I have been with recently
    lead me to be glad
    that there will be "many mansions"
    in your kingdom,
    and that we are likely
    to be in different ones!

When I feel cynical or pessimistic, Lord,
    do help me to be more balanced
    in the way I look at people.
I need to stop judging,
    and stop jumping to conclusions,
    that I may better love others
    in the same generous,
    unprejudiced and even-handed way
    that you love me.
Help me to be more appreciative
    of all that is good
    in every person and in every situation
    - especially when times are difficult.
Amen.

37 - T
HAVE I MISSED OUT?

Lord,
  sometimes I look at others
  and feel a little jealous
  of their talents and abilities.
Sometimes I regret
  having missed
  the opportunities that others have had.
Being with others
  sometimes makes me feel more lonely
  because I feel less "fulfilled"
  than they seem to be.
Melt in my heart, Lord,
  any feelings of bitterness or ill-will,
  and inspire me
  to be generous and positive,
  that I may be better able
  to see the good in others.
Help me to develop
  my own talents and abilities,
  and praise others
  for the good use of theirs.
Lead me to appreciate people more
  for who they are. Amen.

38 - T
WITHOUT YOU WE CAN DO NOTHING

Lord, we call to mind
  the words of the psalmist:
"If the Lord does not build the house,
  then it is in vain that its builders work.
If the Lord does not watch over the city,
  it is in vain that a watchman keeps vigil.
In vain is your earlier rising,
  your going later to rest,
  you who toil for what you eat,
  whilst God pours out his gifts
  on those who are close to him
  whilst they are sleep."
And we recall, Lord,
  that your disciples worked all night
  but caught no fish
  until you came among them.

Inspire and enable us, Lord,
  to live in your presence
  and bear fruit in plenty,
  knowing that, cut off from you,
  we can do nothing. Amen.

(Ps 126/127; Lk 5⁵, Jn 21³; Jn 15⁵)

39 - T
"WHAT DO YOU WANT ME TO DO FOR YOU?"

Lord Jesus, we read in the gospel
  that you spoke individually
  to many people
  and said:

"Be cured";	*Lk 5¹³*
"Get up and walk";	*Lk 5²⁴*
"What do you want to do for you?";	*Mt 20³²*
"Of course I want to cure you: be healed";	*Mt 8³*
"Let what you want be done for you";	*Mt 9²⁹*
"Receive your sight";	*Lk 18⁴²*
"Receive back your hearing";	*Mk 7³⁴*
"Young man, arise";	*Lk 7¹⁵*
"Go, your son will live";	*Jn 4⁵⁰*
"Go, your faith has saved you."	*Mk 10⁵²*

Knowing that you are present in our midst,
  we ask you today
  to touch each one of us individually
  and fulfil our deep-felt needs
  and bring us your healing.
Amen.

40 - T
LIVING THIS DAY

God our Father,
  lead us to find enjoyment and fulfilment
  in our lives today,
  in all the circumstances
  in which you place us,
  and with the people
  whom you entrust to us.

Inspire us
    to seek first your kingdom,
    live joyfully in your presence,
    and grow in your image and likeness.
Empower us with your Spirit
    that we may transform ordinary lives
    and be credible witnesses of your love.
Amen.

41 - T
BALANCE IN MY LIFE

God our Father,
    lead me to grow in faith
    and keep a healthy balance in my life.
Remind me that I need
    to give time and space for myself
    as well as for others.
Inspire me
    to remaining committed in my work,
    sharing quality time with my family,
    and enjoying
    sufficient rest and recreation.
Amen.

42 - T
FEELING WEAK

Lord, you know
    I'm not in the best of form today.
No longer do I feel your inspiration.
In my weakness
    I pray for all the people
    I will meet during this day.
As your ambassador, I am concerned
    that I might present
    a distorted image of you.
So be with me, Lord.
Be the strength in my weakness,
    and give me some inspiration
    and some enthusiasm
    that I may bring your Good News of love
    to those whom I will meet today.
Amen.

43 - T
THE LOW MOMENTS OF THE DAY

Father,
    when things are not going well,
    touch the hearts of all of us,
    that we may see the best in each other.
Alert me
    to different approaches I might take
    and remind me
    to remain positive in attitude,
    treating others with respect.

When things are going well,
    prevent me feeling smug
    or better than someone else,
    and remind me then
    how important it is
    for us to work together
    and support one another. Amen.

44 - T
KINDNESS AND COURAGE

Lord, I ask you to help me
to show kindness in another's trouble,
and courage in my own. Amen
    (phrased from words of Princess Diana)

45 - T
PRIORITIES, AND SUPPORT OF OTHERS

In times of difficulty, Lord,
    inspire us to get our priorities right
    and support others
    with the same care and concern
    that we would like to experience ourselves.
May we learn the lesson
    that as we encourage and support others,
    our own generosity returns to us
    and builds us up
    in times of difficulty.
Amen.

46 - T
THANKS FOR SOMEONE'S SUPPORT

Thanks, Lord,
    for the support given me today.
I wasn't at my best,
    and just spending time having a chat
    left me brighter
    and a little more energetic.
Thanks for all those
    who are ready to give encouragement.
Help me to look outward
    and offer more support to others.
Help me to live positively and cheerfully
    and make the best of each day.
Amen.

47 - T
THOSE WHO LOOK FOR THE BEST IN ME

Lord, I give thanks
    for those who look for the best in me
    and for all whose hearts touch mine
    in love and kindness,
    in encouragement and support.
I place in your care
    those through whom you minister to me.
Bless them
    and fill their lives with your love.
Amen.

48 - T
APPRECIATING EACH OTHER
AS TEACHERS

Lord,
    we ask for your Spirit
    that, as teachers,
    we may minister to each other
    as well as to the young people
    you have entrusted to us.
Lead us to grow
    in appreciation of one another,
    in acceptance and support,
    and with understanding and generosity.

Help us to grow in awareness
    of the feelings and needs of others,
    and inspire us to look beyond ourselves
    in offering kindness and hospitality
    to others. Amen.

FOR CERTAIN OCCASIONS

49- *FCO*
AT THE START OF THE TERM/HALF-TERM

Father,
    at the start of the new *term/half-term*
    we remember the love of our families
    and the companionship and support
    of colleagues.
We rejoice that you have entrusted us
    with the education and care
    of young people,
    and have called us to help others to grow
    in your image and likeness.

Empower us to bring out the best in others
    and express appreciation
    to all who encourage us
    and bring us new life.
Inspire us to be positive in attitude,
    encouraging in words,
    and loving in actions. Amen.

50- *FCO*
AT THE END OF THE TERM/HALF-TERM

Loving Father,
    as we come to the end
    of another *term/half-term*
    we turn to you in confidence
    and place any difficult relationships
    into the healing hands
    of Jesus, your Son.
Enable us to leave behind
    any pain of the past
    and any regrets or bitterness,
    entrusting the past to your mercy,
    the present to your love,
    and the future to your providence.
Help us appreciate more
    the need to keep a good balance
    in our lives.
May the holiday be for us
    a time of rest and recreation
    to help restore us
    and re-create us
    in your image and likeness,
    as we enjoy

more of the love and presence
of our families,
on whom we ask your blessing.
Amen.

51- *FCO*
FIRST ASSEMBLY OF YEAR 7 AT THE START OF THE NEW YEAR

For the following four prayers/reflections, all the teachers of the school may be invited to stand in front of the students or, if there is a possibility of that appearing intimidating, they could sit or stand at right-angles to the body of students, with only the Head/Assistant Head of Year and the Form Tutors standing at the front.

It can leave a lasting impression on the young people if staff are invited to join in the second and the final prayer. It is advisable to have the four prayers printed out for both students and staff to follow, rather than having them on an overhead transparency. It is necessary to give clear information in advance to all the staff.

a) Introduction

I am pleased to welcome each person today
    as a full member of _____.
Many of us
    who have been at _____ for some time
    believe in our hearts
    that Jesus
    is the Way, the Truth and the Life.
As you grow to maturity in your years here
    and come to make
    more and more choices for yourself,
    we would like - alongside your families -
    to help you to come to know
    that Jesus is calling you,
    so that you can choose for yourself
    to accept his invitation and follow him.

(The source of this first reflection is unknown. The name of the school should be inserted.)

b) *Prayer by teachers*
   in front of the new students

Father,
   we pray for your blessing
   on all these young people
   whom you call by name
   and entrust to our care.
May they grow in knowledge and wisdom
   and in faith and understanding,
   showing care and concern for others.
Amen.

c) *Prayer by new students*

Father,
   we ask you to bless us
   as we take a new step in our lives today.
Keep in us
   a sense of wonder at the marvels of life.
Help us to be keen
   to explore the world of knowledge.
Lead us
   to make good use of our talents
   and work well with others.
Bless us
   that we may grow strong in your love,
   and in concern
   for the good of all people.
May we learn from each other
   and grow in friendship
   with Jesus, your Son and our Brother.
Amen.

d) *Blessing by the teachers:*

I thank my God for you
   every time I think of you,
   and every time I pray for you
   I pray with joy.
I pray that your love
   will keep on growing,
   because God loves you
   and calls you by your name.
May you grow in his love. **Amen**
                    (from St Paul: Philippians 1)
(Alternative prayers in place of (d) that could be
used or adapted, would be: 11,12,16,17,20-24,26)

52- *FCO*
WORK EXPERIENCE

Lord Jesus,
   Carpenter of Nazareth,
   we pray today
   for those on Work Experience
   that they will discover
   more of the responsibilities
   as well as the opportunities
   of adult life.
May they value the qualities
   of commitment and punctuality.
May they appreciate the need
   to respect and be courteous
   to each person,
   and build on their skills
   of relating and working with others.
May their experiences lead them
   to gain a wider perspective on life,
   a greater tolerance
   and understanding of others,
   and a determination
   to be faithful to themselves
   and do what is right.
Amen.
                    (Could also adapt 58 re Sport)

53- *FCO*
EXAMS

Lord, we pray for those about to sit exams,
   that they may remain calm and at peace
   so that they may be able
   to make the best use
   of their talents
   and the study they have done
   and the education they have been given.
Let nothing prevent them
   from doing as well as they deserve,
   and may they be ready
   to support and encourage one another.
For our own talents
   and the education and support
   that we receive,
   we give thanks. Amen.

54- FCO
TIME OF REPORTS / BEFORE A PARENTS' EVENING

God our Father,
(making out reports / Parents' Evening)
comes round quickly - too quickly
and, yet again,
there are pressures of time
and other commitments.
Inspire me now and always
to be fair in the comments I make
- whether spoken or written.
If criticism needs to be made,
may it never be of individuals themselves
but only of their attitude or behaviour.
Let me not judge others or criticise them
either for the faults that I have myself
or if, on my part,
I have not contributed positively enough.
Keep my mind focussed,
that I may always look to the positive
and so help to bring out the best
in each person.   Amen.

55- FCO
LEAVERS' DAY/ CERTIFICATE PRESENTA-TION EVENING / GRADUATION

God our Father,
we can look back over the last few years
and recall the friendships
that have formed,
and the good relationships
that have developed.
We give thanks
for all who have enriched our lives
in various ways:
at home, in school,
in church, and in the local community.
We are conscious too, Father,
of mistakes that have been made
and relationships that have gone sour.
We ask for healing
of what has been negative in the past,
as we place ourselves into your hands.

Inspire us in the years ahead
to live in such a way
that we readily apologise
when things go wrong,
as well as
expressing thanks and encouragement
to those who are a part of our lives.
We give thanks, Father,
for the gifts and talents and skills
you have given to each one of us.
We think of people
who may have received less than others
but have made much of themselves.
We remember, too,
those who have overcome
great difficulties,
and all who have inspired us
because they have given of their best.
In giving thanks
for what has been in the past,
we ask for your blessing
on our present and future.
We pray for wisdom
in setting our priorities
and in making our choices,
that we may live fully
and make our part of the world
a better place
because of the care and compassion
that we will bring to it.
We give thanks today
and we commit ourselves
to be people who act justly,
love tenderly
and walk humbly with you, our God.
Amen.   *(The last three lines: cf Micah 6[8])*

56- FCO
PRAYER AT GOVERNORS' MEETINGS

God our Father,
we bring before you
the young people entrusted to our care
as parents, teachers and governors.
We pray for all members

of our school community
that we may work together
to bring out the best in one another,
and develop a true sense of values
through following Jesus,
your Son and our Brother. Amen.

57- *FCO*
BEFORE AN INSPECTION

God our Father,
we have many thoughts and feelings
as the time of Inspection approaches.
We pray
that all that is good about our school
may be appreciated,
and that everyone may be seen
as they give of their best.
May the quality of relationships
be evident,
and the respect
that is given to individuals.
May this time remind us
to value all the more
our need to work together
and support and encourage one another.
Amen.

58- *FCO*
SPORTS DAY

Lord our God,
may the playing
and the watching of sport
remind our young people
of some of the qualities needed
for daily life:
- to use well their skills and talents;
- to grow in respect for other people
and value the good use that others make
of different skills and abilities;
- to learn to work well with others,
appreciating that each
has their own part to play.
Bless them with good health
and a readiness to learn

from life's experiences
of mistakes and "failure" and "success".
May they develop the qualities
of fairness and generosity,
of being positive and enthusiastic,
of having clear goals in mind.
Inspire all of us to be committed
to become more fully alive
so that each of us - working together -
may help to build up your Kingdom.
Amen.

59- *FCO*
JUSTICE AND PEACE

Lord, we remember before you
all our brothers and sisters
who are weighed down with suffering.
Bless and guide us
that your love may be reflected
in our concern for the hungry,
the oppressed and the unloved.
Help us to acknowledge
and grow in appreciation
that all people are made
in your image and likeness.
Amen.

60- *FCO*
LIVING SIMPLY

Lord, may we who have plenty
live simply
so that others may simply live. Amen.

61- *FCO*
MY SMALL SACRIFICE

Lord, as many human hands
transform many grains of wheat
into a loaf of bread,
so may our small sacrifices
help towards the building up
of our human family.
We ask this through Jesus,
who is our brother,
and who fed the hungry. Amen.

62- *FCO*
THOSE WHO ARE SICK, AFRAID, WORRIED

Lord Jesus,
we ask you to bring your healing touch
to those whom we know
to be sick, afraid, or worried.
Bring them your peace and healing.
Amen.

63- *FCO*
IN YOUR OWN WAY, LORD

Lord Jesus,
we ask you to touch *Jenny*
and bring *her* healing
in your own way. Amen.

64- *FCO*
THE ONE YOU LOVE IS ILL

Lord, as your friend Lazarus lay ill,
others remarked to you
that *"the one you love is ill."*
People said: *"See his love for him."*
Today, Lord Jesus,
we pray for _____
because *he* - the one you love - is ill.
We ask you to bring
your healing and peace
to *him* and *his* family. Amen.

(re 'Lazarus', see John 11)

65- *FCO*
FOR SOMEONE WHO HAS DIED

Loving Father,
to you the dead do not die
and, in death, our life is changed
- not ended.
We believe that all that binds us together
in love and friendship
does not end with death.
Hear our prayers for _____
who has died.
As you have made each of us

in your image and likeness
and have called us by name,
hold *him/her* safely in your love
in your kingdom
of light, happiness and peace.
Amen.

66- *FCO*
FOR THE DECEASED AND THOSE WHO MOURN

Father,
your Son declared "blessed"
all those who mourn,
knowing that no-one can mourn
unless they love very much.
Bring courage and strength
to those who now mourn
because they have loved greatly.
In your loving kindness
bring them healing and inner peace,
and lead the one they mourn
into your kingdom
of light, happiness, and peace. Amen.

67- *FCO*
FOR SOMEONE WHOSE RELATIVE/ FRIEND HAS DIED

Lord Jesus, you tell us
that those who mourn are "blessed",
knowing that only those
who love greatly
can mourn.
We know, too,
that it is better
to have loved and lost someone
than never to have loved at all.
Be with _____
and may the members of *his/her* family
be strengthened,
knowing that others care for them
and hold them in prayer. Amen.

(Insert the name of the one
whose relative/friend has died)

184

68- *FCO*
FOR THOSE ABOUT TO BE CONFIRMED

Father,
>we bring before you
>those about to be confirmed.

We ask that the power of the Holy Spirit
>may be in their lives
>so that they may live fully with his gifts
>of wisdom and understanding,
>of knowledge and good judgment,
>of courage and reverence,
>and of wonder and awe in your Presence.

Inspire them to live their faith
>in a genuine and credible way,
>and grow as the people
>you call them to be.

Amen.

69- *FCO*
GENERAL ELECTION / GOVERNMENT

God our Father,
>*(as our General Election approaches)*
>we pray for all
>who *(are/will be)*
>in positions of leadership
>in our country.

We pray that they may live
>as people of integrity and honesty,
>growing in a sense
>of duty and responsibility,
>always being aware of the needy
>and ready to be of service to others.

We pray for ourselves,
>that the Holy Spirit
>may inspire and empower us
>so that our attitude may reflect
>the values of the gospel.

Amen.

70
WELCOME TO A CIVIC DIGNITARY

1   *Mister Mayor,*
>*we would like to welcome you*
>*to our school*
>*which is named after*
>*_____, (Saint or person)*
>*who _____*
>*(did what? Patron saint of?)*

2   *Through you*
>*we would like to thank*
>*_____ Education Authority*
>*who have helped to support our school.*
>*We appreciate our attractive buildings,*
>*but we trust*
>*that we may value **each other***
>*even more.*

3   *We are determined*
>*to look for all that is good*
>*in people and situations,*
>*as we seek*
>*to understand and appreciate*
>*ourselves and others.*

4   *We are committed*
>*to discover and develop our talents,*
>*and value the good use*
>*that others make*
>*of their skills and abilities,*
>*appreciating that each*
>*has our own part to play in life.*

As Mother Teresa often said
>*to those who visited her:*
>*"I cannot do what you do,*
>*and you cannot do what I do,*
>*but together we can do something*
>*beautiful for God."*

5   *As we grow older,*
>*we would like to live in peace,*
>*be happy*
>*and do what is right,*
>*and be responsible citizens*
>*of our town and country.*

6 *This chapel is a place of peace and quiet,*
    a place of prayer.
  It is the centre of our school.
  We would invite you to join us
    as we pray together,
    using the words on the sheet...

7 "Our Father..." *(or use or adapt one of*
  prayers 8,23,24,29,55)

8 *We hope that you will feel*
    particularly welcome
    in our school today.

(The above words should be adapted to local
circumstances and spoken by several young
people or, preferably, new words can be
produced after the ideas of a group are collated,
perhaps including:
- the appreciation that can be expressed via a
civic dignitary,
- what their hopes are for the future,
- how they see their responsibilities, and
- how they might wish to make a statement of
commitment.)

Index

INDEX

Bonhoeffer, Dietrich - 4 Feb; 9 July
Books: burning - 4 May
Bosco, St John - 31 Jan
Bosnia - 28 June; 11 July
Boston - 31 May
Boxing - see Ali, Mohammed
Braille, Louis - 2 Jan
Braveheart - 7 June
Bravery - see 'courage'
Bread - 19 Feb; 16,30 March; 21 July
Breakfast - 19 Feb
Brixham - 17 May
Brontë, Charlotte - 31 March
Bruce, Robert the - 7 June
Bubonic Plague - 12 June
Buddhism - 25 Aug
Building - 26 Feb
Bullimore, Tony - 12 Jan
Bunyan, John - 24 Jan
Busby, Matt - 6 Feb

Caesar - 17 July
CAFOD - 10 April; Family Fast Day, Vol 1
Calculator - 19 June
Calculus - 4 Jan
Calment, Jeanne - 3 Aug
Cana - Shrove Tuesday, Vol 1
Candlemas - 2 Feb
Cardinal - 26 March
Carnarvon, Lord - 16 Feb
Carnegie, Andrew - 10 Aug
Carnival - Shrove Tuesday, Vol 1
Carretto, Carlo - Intro.
Carter, Howard - 16 Feb
Carton, Sydney - 10 June
Cathedrals - 8,9 Feb
Cat's eyes - 3 April
Challenge - 15 Feb
Challenger - 28 Jan
Change - 11 May
Channel, English - 5 May
Channel Islands - 2 July;
Charles II - 5 March
Chernobyl - 26 April

Chesterton, G.K. - Ascension, Vol 2
Chile - 13 March
China - 16 Jan; 24 May
Chinese New Year - 16 Jan
Chocolate - 20 Aug
Choices - 31 May; 6 June; 2,9,12,27 July;
  8 Aug
Chopsticks - 16 April
Christie, Agatha - Intro.
Churchill, WS - 23 Jan, 11 March; 4 June;
  13 July
Church Unity - 18,25 Jan; 8,21 Feb
Circulation - 1 March
Civic dignitary - Vol 2 Appendix of Prayers
  - 70
Civil Rights - see 'human rights'
Civil War, American - 4 March; 9 April
Civil War, Yugoslavia - 11 July
Clarke, Arthur C - 22 July
Clemens, Samuel - see 'Mark Twain'
Coca-Cola - 30 Aug
Coffee - 10 April
Cold War - Easter Sunday, Vol 1; 1 May;
  13 Aug
Collins, Michael (astronaut) - 22,25 July
Colombia - 30 July
Columba, St - 25,27 May
Comets - 8 Jan; 13 April
Commandments - 15 Jan; 8 June; 18 Aug
'Common Good' The- Intro;18 March; 26
  May
Commonwealth - 7 March
Communism - Easter Sunday, Vol 1;
  1,14 May; 11 July; 13 Aug
Compassion - 3 Jan; 5 June
Compliment - 21 April
Concentration camps - 12,22 March;
  9,14 Aug
Confession - 26 March; Shrove Tuesday,
  Vol 1 (see 'Reconciliation')
Confirmation - 23 May; Vol 2 Appendix of
  Prayers - 68
Connery, Sean - 6 March
Conscience - 31 July

Consequences - 26 April *(see also 'choices')*
Cooperation - 21 July
Corn Flakes - 19 Feb
Cornwall - 11 Aug
Corpus Christi - Vol 2
Costner, Kevin - 5 March
Coubertin, Baron Pierre de - 6 April
Country - 20 Jan
Courage - 12 Jan; 15 Feb; 4 March; 4 June;
    8,23 July; 31 Aug; Vol 2 Appendix of
    Prayers - 44; *(see 'disability')*
Creation - 8 Jan, 12 Feb; 1,8,31 March;
    11,12,13 April
Crécy - 12 June
Cricket - 15 March
Crimea - 16 June
Crisps - 28 July
Cross - Good Friday & Easter Sunday, Vol 1;
    Trinity, Vol 2
Crucifix - 26 March
Crum, George - 28 July
Crusades - Good Friday, Vol 1
Cryptogram - 1 Aug
Cuba - 18 Jan
Cunard - 22 Jan
Cup Final - 17 May
Cycle of evil/hatred - 10 May; 18 June;
    11 July; 5,18 Aug
Czar - 17 July

Dachau - 22 March; 9 Aug
Damian, Fr - 19 March
Darkness - 1 Jan, 3 April *(see 'light')*
Darwin, Charles - 12 Feb
David, St - 1 March
Davies, William - 3 July
Da Vinci, Leonardo - Maundy Thursday, Vol 1
D-Day - 4,6 June; 18 Aug
Dead Poets' Society - 7 Jan
Deafness - *(see 'Helen Keller'; & 'A.G.Bell")*;
    Good Friday, Vol 1; 7 May
Death - 6,7 Feb; 21,24 March; 5,8,14,15
    April; 3,8,16,22,25,31 Aug; Vol 2
    Appendix of Prayers 65-67

Decimal currency - 10 Jan
De La Salle, John Baptist - 7 April; 15 May;
    Vol 2 Appendix of Prayers - 32
Denmark - 29 July
Derby - 2 June
Devon - 16 Aug
Diamond (dog) - 20 March
Diana, Princess - 31 Aug; 6 Sept
Dickens, Charles - Intro.; 9,10 June; 26
    July
Differences - 8 Feb
Dillinger, John - 6 July
Disability - 19 Jan; 3 March; 19 July;
    1,3 June *(see also 'illness')*
Disaster - 3,28 Jan; 11,14,15,26 April
Discernment - Vol 2 Appendix of Prayers - 28
Discrimination - *see 'prejudice'*
Dix, Dom Gregory - 'Body & Blood of
    Christ', Vol 2
Dog - 20 March
Door - 1 Jan, 26 Feb
Dream - 4 April
Dunant, JH - 9 May
Dunblane - 3 March *(should refer to 13 March)*
Dunkirk - 4 June
Duties - see *'responsibilities'*
Dying - *see 'Death'*

Easter - Vol 1
Eclipse - 11 Aug
Education - 18 May (prayer), 31 May
Education Reform Act - Intro.
Effort - 13 July
Egypt - 16 Feb
Eichmann, Adolf - 31 May
Einstein, Albert - 14 March; 18 April;
    18 May
Elderly - 3 Aug
Election - 20 Jan; 12 May; Vol 2 Appendix
    of Prayers 69 *(and see 'voting')*
Electricity - 3 Feb
Elijah - Shrove Tuesday, Vol 1
Eliot, TS - 7 Jan; Shrove Tuesday, Vol 1
Elizabeth I, Queen - 23 March; 28,31 July

Elizabeth II, Queen - 20 April; Maundy
    Thursday, Vol 1; 5,29 May; 12 July
Emergency services - 11,12 Jan
    (see also 'disaster')
Emerson, RW - 5 Feb
Emmaus - Intro.; 17 May
Encouragement - 26,27 Jan; 23 Feb;
    Vol 2 Appendix of Prayers - 30
Enemies - 15 Jan
Enola Gay - 6 Aug
Environment - e.g. 12 Feb; 6,16 March;
    (see also 'creation')
Epiphany - 5,6,7 Jan; 25 July
Escobar, Andrés - 30 July
E.T. - 11 June
"Ethnic cleansing" - 11 July
Eucharist - Holy Thursday, Vol 1; 21 July;
    'Body & Blood of Christ', Vol 2
European Union - 7 May; 8 June
Eutychus - 31 July
Everest - 29 May; 24 Aug
Evolution - 12 Feb
Exams - 23 May; Vol 2 Appendix of
    Prayers 53
Exmoor - 16 Aug
Extraordinary - 7 Jan; 20 Aug; *(see also
    'ordinariness')*

Failure *(see 'success')* - 4 March
Fairtrade - 10 April
Faith - 30 June; 25 July; 1,17 Aug
Faithfulness - 13 Feb; 7,20 March
Faiths (other than Christian) - *(see
    'Judaism', 'Islam', 'Buddhism', 'Chinese')*
Family Fast Day - 28 July; Appendix to
    Vols 1 & 3 *(see also 'hunger')*
Fear - 28 Feb; 18 July
Fingerprints - 6 July
Fire - 26 Feb; 20 March; 21 Aug; Pentecost,
    Vol 2; Trinity, Vol 2
First Fridays - 'Body & Blood of Christ',
    Vol 2
First World War - 28 June; 1 July
Fisher, St John - 22 June

Fisherman - 14 July
Five thousand, feeding of - 16 July
Fleming, Dr Alexander - 9 Jan; 11 March
Flower girl - 26 July
Flowers - 15 April
Food - *(see 'hunger')* 16 March; 16 April;
    28 July
Football - 13 Jan; 29 March; 29 April;
    17 May; 2,12,27 June; 30 July
Forgiveness - 17 Jan; 26 Feb; 22,23 March;
    4,11,13,22 May ; 7,17 July
Forrest Gump - 20 Aug
Four-minute mile - 6 May
Francis of Assisi - 5 March
Frank, Anne - 12 March
Frankincense - 7 Jan
Franklin, Benjamin - 17 April
Freedom - *(see 'slavery')*; Trinity, Vol 2
Freeman, Laurence - Intro.
French Revolution - 10 June
Friends - 13 Feb; 23 April; 20 June; 4 July;
    12,18,29 Aug
Gachet, Dr - 16 May
Gagarin, Yuri - 12 April
Gajounicezek, Franz - 14 Aug
Galileo - 8 Jan
Gallipoli - 3 May
Gandhi - 29,30 Jan; 5,17 Feb; 12,17 May;
    28 July; 29 Aug
Garaudy, Roger - 22 May
Garland, Judy - 19 Aug
General Election - 20 Jan; 7 Feb
    (see 'voting')
Genesis - 12 Feb
George, St - 23 April
George II, King - 22 Aug
George IV, King - 26 June
George VI, King - 1,22 Jan
Germs - 15 July
Gibson, Mel - 7 June
Gifts - 5,6,7,20 Jan *(see 'talents')*;
    Pentecost, Vol 2
Gladstone, W.E. - 19 May
Glasgow - 30 May

Loyalty - 13 Feb
Loyola, St Ignatius - *see 'Ignatius'*
Lucas, George - 2 May
Luwum, Janani - 9 July
Lynmouth - 16 Aug
Lyte, Henry - 17 May

Magee, John - 28 Jan
Magna Carta - 15 June
Malta - 25 Jan
Manchester - 1 Aug
Manchester United - 6 Feb
Mandela, Nelson - Intro.; 27 April; 10 May; 12,18 July
Marconi - 27 March
Mardi Gras - Shrove Tuesday, Vol 1
Mark, St - 25 April
Marriage - 17 Aug
Mars - 4 July
Martyrs - 27 May; 20 June; 8 July
Mary (Our Lady) - 2,11,28 Feb; 25 March; 20 May; 15 Aug
Mary, Queen - 22 Jan
Masefield, John - 12 Jan
Mass - *see 'Eucharist'*
Maundy Thursday - Vol 1
Mayor - Vol 2 Appendix of Prayers, 70
M.E. - 19 Feb
Media - 23 May
Meister, Joseph - 15 July
Memories - 5 Jan; 3 Aug
"Messiah, The" - 22 Aug
Mezuzah - 8 Aug
Micah 4 - 27 Feb; 22 April
Michelangelo - 18 Feb
Miracles - 3 May
Misérables, Les - 22,26 May
Mistakes - 4 July *(see also 'forgiveness')*
Mitterand, President - 5 May
Miyashima, Toki - 6 May
Molokai - 19 March
Money - 10 Aug
Monica, St - 28 Aug
Monotheism - 8 Aug

Monument - 26 Feb
Moon - 11,12 April; 20-22, 25 July
Moonlight Sonata - 3 March
Morgan, Charles - Sacred Heart, Vol 2
More, St Thomas - 7 Feb; 5,22 June
Morse Code - 14 April
Moses - Shrove Tuesday, Vol 1
Mount St Helens - 26 Aug
Mourning - 15 April; 17 May; 25 Aug
    (see also 'death')
Multi-cultural - including 16 Jan; 1,2,24,25 Feb; 21,29,30 March; 19 April; 9 May; 8 June; 7 July; 8,25 Aug
Munich - 6 Feb; 9 Aug
Muscles - 17 June
Music - 3 March; 28 April; 7 May; Trinity, Vol 2
Muslim - *see 'Islam'*
'My Fair Lady' - 26 July
Myrrh - 6,7 Jan

Nagasaki - 6 Aug
Name - 22 Jan; 23 Feb; 7,29 April *(see also 'individuality')*
Napoleon - 17 Jan; 8 June
National Anthem - 20 April
National Health Service - 5 July
Nazis - 22 March; 4 May *(& see 'concentration camps', 'Hitler', 'Second World War')*
New Orleans - Shrove Tuesday, Vol 1
Newman, JH - 21 Feb; Good Friday, Vol 1
Newton, Sir Isaac - 4 Jan; 20 March
Newton, John - 24 July
New Year - 1,16 Jan
Niagara Falls - 30 June
Nicholas II, Tsar - 17 July
Niebuhr, Reinhold - 11 May
Nightingale, Florence - 16 June
Nineveh - 2 March
Noah - Shrove Tuesday, Vol 1
Nobel Prize - 14 Jan; 10 May
Nolan, Chris - 19 Jan
Norkay, Tenzing - 29 May

Offering - 14 Jan; 28,30 March; Vol 2
   Appendix of Prayers 4-8
Offertory prayers - 30 March
Olympic Games - 6 April; 19,23 July; 5 Aug
'Only Fools and Horses' - 3 Feb
Opportunities - 9 Jan
Ordinariness - 7 Jan; 1 April; 19 May; 9
   July; 20 Aug
Orthodox, Russian - 25 April; Lent Volume
   1; 17 July
'Our Father' - 1 Aug
Our Lady - see 'Mary'
Owen, Jesse - 5 Aug
Ozanam, F - 23 Aug
Oz, Land of - 19 Aug

Pain - 6 Jan; 25 Aug (see also 'illness')
Pancakes - Shrove Tuesday, Vol 1
Pankhurst, Emmeline - 14 June
Paris - 26 March
Parkinson's Disease - 23 July
Parks, Rosa - 15 Jan
Parliament - 7 Feb
Pascal, Blaise - 19,24 June
Pasteur, Louis - 15,16 July
Patrick, St - 17 March
Paul, Saint - 25,26,27 Jan; 29 June
St Paul's Cathedral - 19,29 May
Paul VI, Pope - Intro.; 8 May; 25 July; 6 Aug
Peace - 23 Jan; 27 Feb; 5,13 March; 9 April;
   5,8,13,27 May; 28 June; 1 July; (see
   also 'Justice' & 'War')
Peenemünde - 18 Aug
Pele - 30 July
Pemberton, Dr J - 30 Aug
Penicillin - 9 Jan
Penn, William - 5 March
Pentecost (Christian) - 18 Jan; Vol 2
Pentecost (Jewish) - 8 June
Peter Pan - 22 Feb
Peter, St - 28 Feb; 29 June
Philippians 4 - 22 Feb
Philip, Prince - 17 July
Philosophers - 5,20 Feb

Phipps, James - 14 May
Pilgrim's Progress - 24 Jan
Pitt, William - 31 July
Pius XII, Pope - 1 May
Plato - Intro.
Pompeii - 24 Aug
Positive - 18 Feb; 10,17,26 June; 2,9 July
   (see also 'best' and 'prejudice')
Possessions - (see 'money'); 14 July; 10 Aug
Potatoes - 28 July
Potts, Lisa - 8 July
Poverty - Family Fast Day, Vol 1
Praying - 1,4,12,15,29 Aug (see 'presence
   of God)
Prejudice - 15,29 Jan; 21 March; 4,30 April;
   10,18 May ; 5,25,27 June; 11 July; 5 Aug
Presence of God - 10,13,24,25 Feb; 8,17,
   26,27,31 March; 1,7,12,22,25 April;
   9,24,28, May; 20 June; 4,24,28 Aug;
   Vol 2 Appendix of Prayers 1-3,27; Ash
   Wed; Palm Sunday; Good Friday;
Presentation - 2 Feb
President - 20 Jan
Priesthood - 4,12,14 Aug
'Prime Suspect' - 21 Aug
Priorities - Family Fast Day, Vol 1; 12,27,
   28 July; 8,10 Aug
Prisoners - 24 Jan; 24 March; 22 May; 20
   June; 12 July; 22 Aug
Prodigal Son - Intro.; Shrove Tuesday, Vol 1;
   19 July
Prophet - 2 March, 22 April
Psalm 8 - 12 April; 20 July; 7 Aug
Psalm 117 - 20 April
Psalm 137 - 25 Feb
Psalm 138/9 - 10,25 Feb
Pullias - Intro.
Pullman - 10 Aug
Pygmalion - 26 July

Quakers - 24 Jan, 5 March
Qualities (see 'talents')
'Quality Street' - 20 Aug
Quiet - 1 April; 12,14,27 July
Qur'an - 19 April

V-1/2 weapons - 18 Aug
Vaccination - 14 May; 15 July
Valentine, St - 14 Feb; Sacred Heart, Vol 2
Valjean, Jean - 22 May
Values - 7 Feb; 30 May; 21 July; 30 Aug
Van Breemen, Peter - Sacred Heart, Vol 2
Van Gogh, Vincent - 16 May; 3 Aug
Vatican Council, Second - 18 Jan
VE Day - 8 May
Vengeance weapons - 18 Aug
Venice - 25 April
Versailles - 28 June
Vesuvius, Mount - 1,24 Aug
Vianney, John - 4 Aug
Victoria, Queen - 21,22 Jan; 9 June;
    15 July; 3 Aug
Vincent de Paul, Society of - 23 Aug
Violence - 29,30 Jan; 30 April; 13 May; 5
    June; 5 Aug; (& see 'war')
Virgin Mary - see 'Mary'
Virus - 14 May
Vision - 2 Jan; 1,16,18,21 Feb; 3 March;
    3,4,5 April; 2,4 May; 21 July; 30 Aug
    (see also 'blindness', 'sight', 'space' &
    'wonder')
Vitality - see 'life-giving','awareness' and
    'healing'
Voltaire - 20 Feb
Voting - 12 May; 14 June; Vol 2 Appendix
    of Prayers - 69
Voyager - 8 Jan
V-weapons - 18 Aug

Waite, Terry - 24 Jan
Wales, Princess of - 31 Aug; 6 Sept
Walker, Peter - Intro.
Wanamaker, Sam/Zoe - 21 Aug
War - see "First W.W" & "Second W.W" &
    Justice; 17,23,28 Jan; 4,27 Feb; 13
    March; 9,30 April; 8,9,31 May; 4,6,28
    June; 1,11 July; 6,18 Aug
Water - 12 Jan; 14 April; 16,21 Aug
Waterloo - 17 Jan; 18 June
Wellesley, Arthur - see 'Wellington'

Wellington - 17 Jan; 18 June
Westminster Abbey - 9,29 July
Whale - 2 March
Wheat - 19 Feb, 16 March
Whispering Gallery - 19 May
Whitman, Walt - 26 May
Whitsun - see Pentecost
Wilberforce, William - 29 July
William III, King - 13 Feb; 31 July
Wind - Pentecost, Vol 2
Wind in Willows, The - 8 March
Windows - 31 July
Wine - 30 March; 15 July
Wisdom - 4,7,9 Jan ; 11,18 May; 4,16, 25
    July; Vol 2 Appendix of Prayers - 16
Witness - 17 Feb; 8 July (see 'Martyr')
Wizard of Oz - 19 Aug
Wonder - 8 Jan; 10,12,16 Feb; 8,14
    March; 11,12,13 April; 1 June; 3,22
    July; 2 Aug (see also Introduction
    'appreciation', 'creation' and 'space');
    Vol 2 Appendix of Prayers
Work - 11 Jan; 18 March; 1 May; 14 July;
    23 Aug; Vol 2 Appendix of Prayers -
    e.g. 52
World - 29 March
World Cup - 30 July
Wren, Sir Christopher - 26 Feb

X-rays - 10 Feb

Year - 1,16 Jan
Yeltsin, Boris - 17 July

Zacchaeus - 23 Feb; 29 April; 11 June